Crochet This!

Crochet This!

STEP-BY-STEP TECHNIQUES

65 ESSENTIAL STITCHES • MORE THAN 25 PROJECTS

sixth&springbooks

sixth&springbooks

104 West 27th Street
New York, NY 10001

Connect with us on Facebook at facebook.com/sixthandspringbooks

Senior Editor
MICHELLE BREDESON

Art Director
JOE VIOR

Production
J. ARTHUR MEDIA

Chief Executive Officer
CAROLINE KILMER

Production Manager
DAVID JOINNIDES

President
ART JOINNIDES

Chairman
JAY STEIN

Photography Credits
PAUL AMATO: pages 22, 97, 105, 107, 153, 155, 161
ROSE CALLAHAN: pages 90, 93, 95, 99, 101, 103,
109, 113, 115, 117, 119, 121, 123, 125, 127, 129, 131,
133, 137, 139, 141, 143, 145, 148, 149, 151, 157,
159, 164, 165, 167, 171, back cover
JACK DEUTSCH: cover, pages 6–7, 38, 174–176
MARCUS TULLIS: pages 40–89

Library of Congress Cataloging-in-Publication Data

Title: Crochet this! : step-by-step techniques,
65 essential stitches,   more than 25 projects.
Description: First edition. | New York :
Sixth&Spring Books, 2019. | Includes index.
Identifiers: LCCN 2019014654 | ISBN 9781640210486 (pbk.)
Subjects: LCSH: Crocheting.
Classification: LCC TT825 .C751877 2019 | DDC 746.43/4--dc23
LC record available at https://lccn.loc.gov/2019014654

Manufactured in China

1 3 5 7 9 10 8 6 4 2

First Edition

CONTENTS

INTRODUCTION

To the uninitiated, crochet can seem like a magic act. With just a simple hook and some yarn, experienced stitchers conjure up everything from cozy afghans to runway-ready fashions—seemingly out of thin air. But unlike magicians, crocheters love to share their secrets. And once you know the basics, crochet really isn't as puzzling as it may seem. *Crochet This!* takes the mystery out of crochet.

We start right at the beginning. In the first section, Techniques Step by Step, you'll learn how to create the foundation of all crochet projects (the foundation chain); how to work basic stitches you'll use over and over; finishing techniques, such as seaming, buttonholes, and embellishments; and how to decipher crochet stitch diagrams.

The second part of this book, Stitch Dictionary, is a resource you'll turn to again and again in your crochet journey. Whether you use a single pattern to create a simple design, such as a blanket or scarf, arrange motifs in any number of combinations to design your own projects, or finish your projects with a crocheted edging or embellishment, you'll find no shortage of inspiration. It's organized by type of stitch for easy reference, and all of the patterns include written instructions and charts.

Finally, the Projects section presents a gorgeous collection of twenty-seven crochet projects from some of today's top crochet designers. There are projects that are easy enough for beginners and ones that will challenge more experienced stitchers. The timeless designs include an infinity scarf that features a simple, but elegant lace stitch from Yoko Hatta; a quick-stitch bobbled slouch hat from Candi Jensen; a vibrant beach bag from Robyn Chachula that showcases the Bruges technique; a lacy jacket from Deborah Newton that will become a modern classic; and many more.

Whether you've never picked up a hook or you're looking for inspiration and fun stitches and projects to tackle, *Crochet This!* will be an essential part of your crocheter's bag of tricks.

TECHNIQUES
STEP-BY-STEP

From holding the hook, to creating essential stitches,
to finishing your projects for a professional look,
the step-by-step instructions and photos in this section
will have you covered.

ON THE HOOK

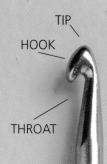

TIP

HOOK

THROAT

SHAFT

HANDLE

Hooks are the key component to crochet construction. They come in two classifications: **yarn hooks**, which are used for projects made with yarn, and **steel hooks**, which are used solely with crochet thread for lacemaking and filet techniques. Both styles are comprised of different sections: the tip and throat (the hooked end), which are used to make the stitch, the shaft, which determines the size of the hook, and the handle, which is used to hold the hook.

Yarn hooks can be found in aluminum, plastic, and acrylic or in natural materials such as wood, bamboo, and bone. Some have ergonomically shaped handles and cushioned grips that make them comfortable to hold and easier to work with. Start with the old-fashioned aluminum style and as you gain skill and confidence, try experimenting with other styles to see which you like best.

The size of the hook (in combination with the yarn you are using for the project) will determine the size of your stitches. On most hooks, you'll find the size stamped on the handle. In the U.S., hooks are sized by letter of the alphabet, except for size 7. As the letter goes up, so does the size of the hook. Steel hooks are sized by number and reverse the equation; the larger the number, the smaller the hook. The number next to the letter is the equivalent knitting needle size. Generally, smaller hooks are used with thinner yarns and vice versa. The yarn industry has taken some of the confusion out of matching yarn to hook by setting up a standardized system of weights and categories (see page 35).

CROCHET HOOKS

U.S.	Metric
0	2mm
B/1	2.25mm
C/2	2.75mm
D/3	3.25mm
E/4	3.5mm
F/5	3.75mm
G/6	4mm
7	4.5mm
H/8	5mm
I/9	5.5mm
J/10	6mm
K/10½	6.5mm
L/11	8mm
M/13	9mm
N/15	10mm
17	12.75mm
P/19	15mm
S/35	19mm

HOLDING THE HOOK

The first thing you are going to have to do is learn to hold the hook properly. Take your pick from one of these two methods:

The **knife grip** is the most recommended. With the tip and throat facing you, put your dominant thumb flat on the front of the grip and your index finger flat on the back. Now wrap your remaining fingers around the handle.

Your second choice is the **pencil grip**, which looks a little more elegant, but is not quite as comfortable and is prone to putting strain on your hands. With that caveat, here's how it works: hold the hook between your dominant thumb and index finger with the remaining fingers folded down, just as you would a pencil.

GETTING STARTED

Before you jump into making your first crochet project, you need to try out a few basics, from getting the yarn on the hook, to making your first most-basic stitch, to fastening off your stitches.

MAKING A SLIP KNOT

Once you've figured out how to hold the hook you are ready to put it together with your yarn. It all begins with a **slip knot**, the little loop that anchors the yarn to the hook. First, make a loop, placing one end of the yarn centered underneath the loop. (The result, if flattened, will look like a pretzel.) Next, insert the hook under the center strand and pull it up into a loop on the hook (see photo). Pull both yarn ends to tighten the knot on the hook.

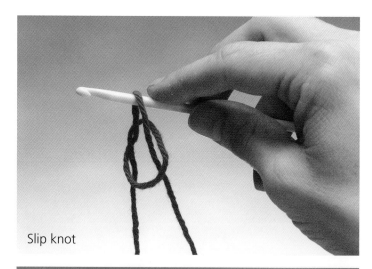

Slip knot

THE FOUNDATION CHAIN

After you get the yarn on the hook, you need to lay the **foundation chain (ch)** for all those stitches to come. This is simply a series of **loops**, called **chain (ch) stitches**, that link together.

A **foundation chain (ch)** has two sides. The side facing as you chain (ch) is called the **top**. And along the top the stitches form a line of little "V"s, and each "V" has two strands: the strand that's nearest you (the right) is called the **front loop**, the strand farthest from you (the left) is called the **back loop**. The new stitches you form will be worked into these loops.

1. To begin the foundation chain, lay the long end of the yarn over the hook from back to front.

The side opposite the top is called the **bottom**. On the bottom, the chain (ch) stitches form a single line of bumps. They are called the **bottom loops**. You may encounter projects that call for crocheting into the bottom loops.

2. Catch the yarn under the hook and draw the yarn through the loop.

COUNTING CHAINS

When you count crochet stitches (and you'll be doing this a lot) always count from the first stitch after the hook to the last stitch before the slip knot. In other words, the loop that's on the hook is *not* counted as a chain (ch) stitch, nor is the slip knot. We'll make it a bit clearer with the illustration on the right.

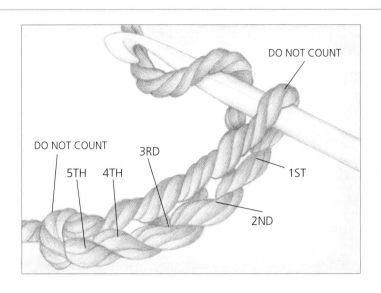

THE FIRST STITCH: SINGLE CROCHET

Now we're going to show you that most basic of crochet stitches, the single crochet (sc).

Start by making a foundation chain (ch) of 11 stitches, holding the **foundation chain (ch)** so that the top is facing you and your thumb and middle finger are holding the third stitch from the hook. Now follow the pictures and instructions below and we'll get you going.

1. Insert the hook under both the front and the back loops of the second chain (ch) from the hook. Wrap the yarn over the hook from back to front—this is called a **yarn-over (yo)**—and catch it on the hook. Now draw the hook through the two chain (ch) stitch loops. You will now have two loops on the hook.

2. Wrap the yarn over the hook from the back to the front—yarn over (yo)—then draw the yarn-over through both loops on the hook.

3. You have now completed one **single crochet (sc)** stitch. Now repeat steps 1 and 2 nine more times, inserting the hook into each chain (ch) stitch across. You will now have ten single crochet (sc) stitches completed across the row.

TURNING CHAIN

Now it's time to move on to the next row. Make one chain (ch) stitch—this is called the **turning chain (ch)**]—then turn the piece from the right to the left. In crochet lingo this is called "chain and turn." For the next row, insert the hook under both the front and the back loops of the first stitch (skipping the one turning stitch). Repeat these steps until you have completed ten rows of single crochet (sc).

FASTENING OFF

When you've completed the number of rows or achieved the length called for in your pattern instructions, you'll need to secure the last stitch so that all your hard work doesn't unravel. This is called **fastening off**, and it's very easy to do.

1. Start by cutting the yarn about 12"/30.5cm from the last loop on the hook. Bring the remaining yarn over the hook.

2. Draw the tail all the way through the loop on the hook. Pull the tail to tighten. Your stitches are now safe and secure.

JOINING YARNS

Unless you make only very small projects, you will likely need to join a new ball of yarn. You also need to join yarn when you change colors.

JOINING AT THE END OF A ROW

As with knitting, you'll usually want to join your yarn at the end of a row—especially if you're working an open-work or lace stitch where there's no way to weave the ends in invisibly. You may lose some yarn from the previous ball, but you can always use that for seaming, fringe, or tassels. Here's how it works. To join a new ball of yarn at the side edge, tie it loosely around the old yarn, leaving at least a 6"/15cm tail. Untie the knot later and weave the ends into the seam.

JOINING YARN MIDROW

There are times when you may need or want to join yarn midrow. Before joining the new yarn midrow, complete the last stitch that you were working on. Tie the old and new together loosely close to the last stitch; yarn tails should be at least 6"/15cm long. Later, untie the knot and weave in the ends under the stitches.

KEEP STITCHING

You can single crochet (sc) your way through any number of fabulous projects, but let's expand our skills a bit. The stitches we're going to introduce here take a little more practice and concentration than single crochet (sc), but they're still pretty basic and are used in many crochet patterns.

WHERE TO START

Each of these stitches gets progressively taller. This is important to understand because which chain (ch) stitch you dip into to make your first crochet stitch will depend on the height of the finished stitch. So because one chain (ch) stitch equals the height of a single crochet (sc) stitch (which we'll cover in a minute),

you'll make your first stitch into the second chain (ch) stitch from the hook. For a half double crochet (hdc) stitch, you'll need two chain (ch) stitches to equal the height, so you will dip your hook into the third stitch from the hook. Confused? Don't worry. The pattern directions will always tell you where to begin.

HALF DOUBLE CROCHET

Remember how we told you crochet stitches kind of build on each other in height? Well, we're going to put that theory into practice with a few new stitches.

The first stitch we'll try is called **half double crochet (hdc)**. To begin, create a foundation chain (ch) with 12 chain (ch) stitches.

1. To begin a half double crochet (hdc) stitch, yarn over (yo).

2. Insert hook under the top 2 loops of the next stitch and yarn over (yo).

3. Draw yarn-over (yo) through stitch; yarn over (yo) again.

4. Draw yarn-over (yo) through all 3 loops on hook.

DOUBLE CROCHET

The **double crochet (dc)** stitch adds one more step to those you've completed in the half double crochet (hdc) (which, by the way, is how the half double got its name). Let's start by making a foundation chain (ch) of 13 stitches, then follow the pictures below.

1. To begin a double crochet (dc) stitch, yarn over.

2. Insert hook under the 2 top loops of the next stitch and yarn over (yo) again.

3. Draw the yarn-over (yo) through the stitch—3 loops are on hook; yarn over (yo) again.

4. Draw yarn-over (yo) through first 2 loops; yarn over (yo).

5. Draw yarn-over (yo) through last 2 loops on hook.

TREBLE CROCHET

The next stitch we'd like you to meet is the **treble crochet (tr)**. This one builds on the double crochet (dc) stitch you learned earlier. To begin your first practice row, make a foundation chain (ch) of 14 stitches, then follow these easy steps.

1. To begin a treble crochet (tr) stitch, yarn over (yo) twice.

2. Insert hook under the 2 top loops of the next stitch and yarn over (yo) once again.

3. Draw yarn-over through the stitch; yarn over (yo) again.

4. Draw yarn-over (yo) through first 2 loops on hook; yarn over (yo) once again.

5. Draw yarn-over (yo) through next 2 loops, yarn over.

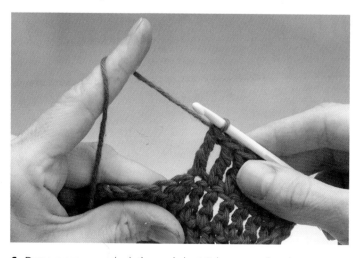

6. Draw yarn-over (yo) through last 2 loops on hook.

SLIP STITCH

While you will occasionally see **slip stitch (sl st)** used in pattern stitches, it is never worked on its own in multiple rows. Instead, it's is used to anchor chain (ch) stitches, shape pieces, make cording, join stitches when working in the round, secure seams, finish edges, and a whole lot more. To try this out, make a foundation chain (ch) of 11 stitches, then follow the simple steps below.

1. Insert the hook under both loops of the second chain from the hook. Yarn over (yo) the hook. Our sample shows working a slip stitch (sl st) into a row of single crochet (sc).

2. Draw through the chain (ch) stitch, then the loop on the hook in one movement. You've made one slip stitch (sl st).

GAUGE SWATCH

Before you dive in to starting a project, you should make yourself a **gauge swatch**, which is a test run of how your pattern, yarn, hook, and stitching style all work together. Start by gathering up the exact yarn and needles you intend to use for the project. Chain (ch) enough stitches to create a square at least 4"/10cm wide. Anywhere from 12 to 20 depending on the size of the hook and the thickness of the yarn you are using should do it. Then work in the specified pattern until the square is a little more than 4"/10cm high.

Put the swatch down on a table or other smooth, hard surface. Use a tape measure or ruler to measure 4"/10cm across the swatch. Count the number of stitches in those 4"/10cm. This will give you the number of stitches.

Now, measure from the bottom to the top of the swatch and count the number of rows in those 4"/10cm. This will give you the number of rows.

Compare these numbers to those in the gauge given for your pattern. If they match, you are ready to get started! If they don't, you'll have to change your hook size and try again. If you were short a few stitches, try using a smaller hook, and if you had too many stitches, try using a larger hook. Try different hook sizes until you get the correct gauge.

INCREASING

Unless you only want to crochet scarves and belts, you'll need to learn to add and subtract stitches, known as increasing and decreasing. Let's start with the increase.

INCREASING IN THE ROW

There are several ways to add stitches to your row; which method you use depends on where the stitch is being added. Really this is nothing more than working 2 or more stitches into one stitch. Simply work 2 stitches into the first stitch and 2 stitches into the last stitch. You have now increased 1 stitch at each side of the row.

INCREASING AT THE BEGINNING OF A ROW

You'll use this method when you need to add a stitch or two at the start of a row.

1. Make the number of chain (ch) stitches you need to increase, then chain (ch) for the height of the stitches you are working in. Here, 3 stitches are going to be increased at the beginning of a single crochet (sc) row, so chain (ch) 3 for the increase and chain (ch) 1 for the height of the single crochet (sc) stitch—4 chain (ch) stitches in total.

2. Work 1 single crochet (sc) in the 2nd chain (ch) from the hook, then work 1 single crochet (sc) in each of the next 2 chain (ch) stitches—3 single crochet (sc) stitches made. Continue to work across the rest of the row.

INCREASING AT THE END OF THE ROW

When you need to add stitches at the end of a row, follow these steps.

1. To make the first increase stitch, insert the hook under the left vertical strand of the last single crochet (sc) stitch. Yarn over (yo) and draw up a loop. Yarn over (yo) and draw through both loops on the hook to complete the new single crochet (sc) stitch.

2. To make the next and all following increase stitches, insert the hook under the left vertical strand of the last single crochet (sc) stitch made. Yarn over (yo) and draw through both loops on the hook to complete the new single crochet (sc) stitch.

DECREASING

Now, let's move on to the decrease. As with the increase, you can do this several ways, each dependent on where the stitches need to be taken away.

DECREASING IN THE ROW

When you need to decrease the number of stitches at the end of a row, the idea is to work each stitch to within the last step to complete it, leaving the last loop (or loops) on the hook. You then yarn over (yo) and draw through all the loops on the hook to combine two (or more) stitches into one. Let's go through it step by step.

DECREASING 1 SINGLE CROCHET

1. Insert the hook into the next stitch and draw up a loop. Insert the hook into the following stitch and draw up a loop.

2. Yarn over (yo) and draw through all 3 loops on the hook. One single crochet (sc) stitch is decreased.

DECREASING 1 HALF DOUBLE CROCHET

1. Yarn over (yo), insert the hook into the next stitch and draw up a loop. Yarn over (yo), insert the hook into the following stitch, and draw up a loop.

2. Yarn over (yo) and draw through all 5 loops on the hook. One half double crochet (hdc) stitch is decreased.

DECREASING 1 DOUBLE CROCHET

1. [Yarn over (yo). Insert the hook into the next stitch and draw up a loop. Yarn over (yo) and draw through 2 loops on the hook] twice.

2. Draw yarn-over (yo) through all 3 loops on the hook. One double crochet (dc) stitch has been decreased.

DECREASING 1 TREBLE CROCHET

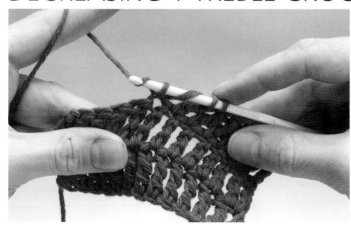 

1. *Yarn over (yo) the hook twice. Insert the hook into the next stitch and draw up a loop. Yarn over (yo), draw through 2 loops on the hook, then yarn over (yo) again and draw through 2 loops on the hook*. Repeat from * to * in the following stitch.

2. Yarn over (yo) and draw through all 3 loops on the hook. One treble crochet (tr) stitch has been decreased.

DECREASING AT THE BEGINNING OF A ROW

If you need to eliminate stitches at the beginning or end of a row, do it like this: Complete the last row before the decrease, then just turn the work (don't chain!). Work 1 slip stitch (sl st) in each stitch that is to be decreased. Then chain (ch) for the height of the stitch you are working in (1 for single, 2 for half double, etc.) and continue to work across the row.

DECREASING AT THE END OF A ROW

If your stitches need to be eliminated at the end of a row, work across the row to the last number of stitches to be decreased and leave them unworked. Chain (ch) and turn to work the next row.

CROCHETING IN THE ROUND

Up to this point we've been stitching in rows. Now, let's try crocheting in the round. To do this you can work in a spiral or joined rounds. These two techniques pave the way for a world of crochet possibilities: hats, bags, the ever-popular granny square. Rounds can shape up into a single item or you can connect smaller ones to create a patchwork piece. You can also use them to make flowers, mandalas, and more.

MAKE A RING

No matter what you're making or which method you're using, all rounds start with a **ring**. Whether that ring is a tightly closed circle (the crown of a hat, for example) or an open tube (say, a sleeve cuff) depends on the number of chain (ch) stitches you start with. We'll demonstrate with a tight start.

1. To make a practice ring, chain (ch) 6. Insert the hook through both loops of the first chain (ch) stitch made. Yarn over (yo) and draw through the chain (ch) stitch and the loop on the hook in one movement.

2. You have now joined the chain (ch) with a slip stitch (sl st) and formed a ring.

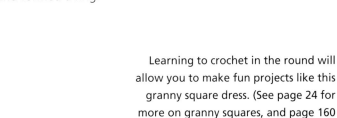

Learning to crochet in the round will allow you to make fun projects like this granny square dress. (See page 24 for more on granny squares, and page 160 for project instructions.)

SPIRALING

Spirals are worked around and around without interruption, usually in single (sc) or half double (hdc) crochet (this is so there won't be a big difference in height at the beginning and end of the round).

1. Chain (ch) 5. Join the chain (ch) with a slip stitch (sl st), forming a ring. Work 10 single crochets (sc) into the ring. Fasten a safety pin in the last stitch made to indicate the end of a round.

2. Work 2 single crochets (sc) in each of the first 9 stitches. Unfasten the safety pin from the last stitch. Work 2 single crochets (sc) in the last stitch. Refasten the safety pin in the last stitch made—you now have 20 stitches. To practice one more round, *work 1 single crochet (sc) in the next stitch, then work 2 single crochets (sc) in the following stitch. Repeat from the * to the end of the round, unfastening, then refastening, the safety pin in the last stitch—you now have 30 stitches.

TIP

It can be tricky to keep track of increases from one round to the next. Use a split-ring marker to mark the end of each round and keep count on a pad of paper as you go.

WORKING JOINED ROUNDS

Joined rounds can be used for any height stitch because the beginning and end of each round is always equal in height. Essentially a series of concentric circles, each round begins with chain (ch) stitches that equal the height of the stitch being used. A slip stitch (sl st) in the first stitch joins the round and completes the circle. It's a little harder to work than a spiral, but because you can see where each round begins and ends, it's also easier to keep track of your increases.

1. Chain (ch) 5. Join the chain (ch) with a slip stitch (sl st), foming a ring. Chain (ch) 3; this equals the height of a double crochet (dc) stitch. Work 12 double crochets (dc) in the ring, then join the round with a slip stitch (sl st) in the top 2 loops of the first stitch.

2. For the second round, chain (ch) 3. Work 2 double crochet (dc) in each of the 12 stitches. Join the round with a slip stitch (sl st) in the first stitch—you now have 24 stitches. To practice one more round, chain (ch) 3, *work 1 double crochet (dc) in the next stitch, then work 2 double crochet (dc) in the following stitch. Repeat from the * to the end of the round. Join the round with a slip stitch (sl st) in the first stitch—you now have 36 stitches.

GRANNY SQUARES

The **granny square** is the motif most people visualize when you mention the word *crochet*. We'll bet almost everyone you know has an afghan their grandma made them using this nifty variation on the basic crochet round. And like most grannies, it can do a lot of things you never expected. Here's how it works.

1. With the first color, ch 4. Join ch with a sl st forming a ring. For round 1, ch 3 (counts as 1 dc), working in the ring, work 2 more dc for the first 3-dc group as shown, then ch 2 for the first corner ch-2 sp.

2. To complete the round, [work 3 dc in ring, ch 2] 3 times. This gives you three more 3-dc groups and three more corner ch-2 sps. Join the rnd with a sl st in the top of the beg ch-3 (the first "dc"). Fasten off.

3. From the RS, join the next color in any corner ch-2 sp with a sl st. (Note: Always alternate the corner you join the color in, so joins are evenly distributed.)

4. For round 2, ch 3 (counts as 1 dc), work 2 dc in the same ch-2 sp (this forms the first half of the first corner), ch 1, [work (3 dc, ch 2, 3 dc) in next ch-2 sp, ch 1] 3 times, at the end work 3 dc in beg ch-2 sp, ch 2 (this forms the second half of the first corner). Join the rnd with a sl st in the top of the beg ch-3. Fasten off. You now have 4 ch-2 corner sps and 4 ch-1 sps (one on each side).

5. Join the next color with a sl st in any corner ch-2 sp. For round 3, ch 3, work 2 dc in same ch-2 sp, ch 1, [work 3 dc in next ch-1 sp, ch 1, work (3 dc, ch 2, 3 dc) in next ch-2 sp, ch 1] 3 times, end work 3 dc in next ch-1 sp, ch 1, work 3 dc in beg ch-2 sp, ch 2. Join rnd with a sl st in top of beg ch-3. Fasten off. You still have 4 ch-2 corner sps, but now you have 8 ch-1 sps (two on each side). For every round that follows, you will increase one ch-1 sp on each side.

TIP

As you crochet around, work the dc groups over the tail of the ring or tail from the previous round so you won't have to weave it in later.

SIMPLE FLOWER HOW-TO

You can change yarns and colors within rounds to create some pretty striking pieces that can be used on their own or stitched together to make a larger piece of fabric. Here's how to create a fab flower.

1. To begin this flower, chain (ch) 5. Insert crochet hook into first chain made, as shown at left. Then yarn over (yo) the hook, pull up a loop, and pull through the loop on the hook to make a ring.

2. To make the first round, chain (ch) 3, which counts as the first half double crochet (hdc) and chain (ch) 1; continue to work [1 half double crochet (hdc) and chain (ch) 1] 11 times. You will have 12 half double crochet (hdc) and 12 chain-1 (ch-1) spaces. Join the round by working a slip stitch (sl st) into the second chain (ch) of the beginning chain-3 (ch-3).

3. Shown here is round 3, or the last round. By working [1 single crochet (sc), 2 half double crochet (hdc) and 1 single crochet (sc)] into each chain-1 (ch-1) space from the previous round, you create a ruffled edge.

FINISHING

Once you finish a project or pieces of a larger project, there are some important steps to take to finish them off properly and give them a professional look: weaving in ends and blocking. And most patterns call for some kind of finish along the edge of your hem, cuff, or collar. This can be done with the exact same yarn, a contrasting color, or a completely different fiber.

WEAVING IN ENDS

When you join a new ball of yarn or change colors, you'll be left with lots of loose ends that need to be woven in. For threads left hanging at the sides of the work, untie the knot you made when joining the yarn and thread one loose strand into a yarn needle. Insert the needle down through the side edge for about 1½"/4cm, then snip off the excess. Thread the remaining strand through the needle and weave it up in the opposite direction. If you changed yarns midrow, push the knot to the wrong side of the fabric. Carefully untie the knot, thread one end of the yarn on a yarn needle, and weave the needle horizontally to the right for about three stitches (make sure the weave doesn't show on the right side). Pull the needle through, then take one small backstitch to secure the yarn. Then snip off the excess. Do the same for the remaining loose end, weaving it to the left.

BLOCKING

Blocking is the process of wetting, pressing, or steaming finished crocheted pieces to give them their permanent size and shape and set the stitches. Most pieces should be blocked before seaming to flatten and smooth the edges and even out the stitches.

Before blocking, read the instructions on the yarn label about fabric care. If you're uncertain how a yarn will react when blocked, experiment with a swatch. You can either wet block or steam block your pieces. To **wet block**, submerge the pieces in cool water for at least 30 minutes. Drain the water and squeeze gently to remove most of the water. Gently roll in a towel to remove excess water. Pin the pieces to a flat surface (such as an ironing board) or blocking board with rustproof pins, gently positioning them to the desired shape and measurements. Allow the pieces to dry completely. You can also **steam block** with an iron or handheld steamer. Hold the steamer or iron above the piece and slowly work over the entire area, letting the steam dampen each piece completely. To protect the piece from intense heat, use a pressing cloth.

CROCHETING ACROSS THE SIDE EDGE

When working vertically, crochet stitches directly into the stitches at the side edge. Not only should you make sure to space them evenly, but go into the stitches at the same depth so that all stitches are the same size. If the edging is being added in preparation for seaming (like afghan squares), also take care to work an equal number of edge stitches on all pieces so they'll all match up perfectly.

CROCHETING ACROSS THE BOTTOM EDGE

When working across the bottom edge, work each stitch between two stitches rather than working into the bottom loops of the foundation chain (ch). (Note: Working through the bottom loops will add length, so only work through them when directions tell you to.)

MARKING A CURVED EDGE FOR SPACING STITCHES

Adding an edging to a curved edge, such as a neckline, will take a little more concentration. The basic technique is the same, but the even distribution of stitches becomes even more critical. Here's how to mark for a perfect finish.

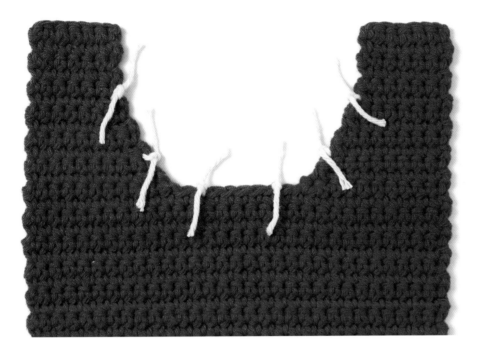

Stitches must be distributed evenly so a trim, neckband, or collar will not flare out or pull in. Place pins, safety pins, or yarn markers, as shown, every 2"/5cm. If you know the number of stitches to be crocheted, divide this by the number of sections marked to determine how many stitches to work between each pair of markers. If no number is given in the directions, use the marked sections to ensure even spacing around the neck.

Adding an edging to a neckline gives a sweater a polished look. (See page 96 for the Lacy Jacket pattern, above, and page 131 for the Pineapple-Stitch Dolman, below.)

TIP

If you're using a thinner yarn to work your edging, you will probably need a smaller hook than the one used for your project. To get things to come out evenly, you'll need to work one stitch in some stitches and two stitches in others. If you're using a thicker yarn, you'll need to use a larger hook and work one stitch in some stitches and skip others. You may have to rip out and start over a few times, but with practice you'll get the hang of it.

SEAMING

Once all of the individual pieces for a project are finished, ends are woven in, and the pieces are blocked, it's time to join them together. This can be done by sewing, weaving, or crocheting them to one another. Your pattern instructions may specify a certain method; if not, choose the one you think will suit the project best. Here are a few of our favorites.

WOVEN SEAM

1. This method gives you an invisible seam with no bulk. Work on a flat surface. With the right sides of both pieces facing you, butt the two edges and secure with safety pins every 2"/5cm. Thread a yarn needle with the tail from the foundation chain. To secure the edges together before weaving, insert the needle from back to front into the corner stitch of the piece without the tail. Making a figure eight with the yarn, insert the needle, from back to front, into the stitch with the tail. Tighten to close up the gap.

2. To begin weaving the seam, insert the needle through the first stitch on the left edge and then through the first stitch on the right edge. Insert the needle through the next stitch on the left edge and then through the next stitch on the right edge. Continue to alternate weaving from edge to edge in this manner, carefully matching stitches (or rows), and drawing the yarn only tight enough the keep the edges together.

BACKSTITCH SEAM

1. The backstitch is used when you need a seam that's extra strong and bulk is not an issue. Place the pieces together so the right sides are facing, then pin every 2"/5cm. Thread the tail from the foundation chain (ch) into the yarn needle. Working from back to front, secure the beginning of the seam by taking the needle twice around the bottom edges. Working from back to front again, insert the needle so it exits about ¼"/5mm from the last stitch, as shown.

2. Insert the needle into the same hole as the last stitch, then back up approximately ¼"/5mm in front of the last stitch. Draw the yarn through, then tighten only enough to keep the edges together. Continue to work in this manner, taking care to keep the stitches the same length and straight.

WHIPSTITCH SEAM

The whipstitch is used for joining squares for an afghan together, like grannies, as well as other short straight edges. Thread the tail from the foundation chain (ch) in a yarn needle. Place the pieces together so the wrong sides are facing, edges are even, and stitches line up. Insert the needle into the back loop of the piece in front and into the front loop of the adjacent stitch of the piece in back. Continue to work in this manner, drawing the yarn only tight enough to keep the edges together.

SINGLE CROCHET SEAM

1. Use this method for decorative exterior seams. Working from the ball of yarn, make a slip knot 6"/15cm from the yarn end. Place the slip knot on the hook. To work across top edges, place the pieces together so wrong sides are facing. Working from front to back, insert the crochet hook through both loops of each piece and draw through a loop. Yarn over (yo) and draw through both loops on hook. Continue to work one single crochet (sc) in each pair of adjacent loops across.

2. To work across side edges, place the pieces together so wrong sides are facing. Working through both thicknesses, work single crochet (sc) stitches directly into matching stitches at the side edge, making sure to space them evenly and at the same depth so that all single crochet (sc) stitches are the same size.

SLIP STITCH SEAM

Use this technique when you want an especially sturdy join, but don't mind the extra bulk. Place the pieces together right sides facing and edges even; pin every 2"/5cm. Working through both thicknesses and from front to back, insert the crochet hook between the first two stitches, one stitch in from the edge. Working from the ball of yarn, catch the yarn on the wrong side (about 6"/15cm from the end) and draw through a loop. *Insert the hook between the next two stitches. Draw through a loop, then draw through the loop on the hook. Repeat from the *, keeping an even tension on the yarn so the stitches are even in size and the joining has the same stretchiness as the crocheted fabric.

BUTTONHOLES

When you begin crocheting sweaters and other garments, you'll need to know how to create button-holes that complement the project. A two-row buttonhole is basically a hole you insert a button into. Button loops give a very feminine feel to a sweater; they're also sweet on baby things.

TWO-ROW BUTTONHOLE

The two-row buttonhole is the most common. It can also accommodate just about any size button. Here's how to work it.

1. Work to the placement marker of the buttonhole—single crochet (sc) is shown here. Chain (ch) 3 (not too loosely), skip the next 3 stitches, then continue to work to the end of the row or to the next marker.

2. On the next row, work to the chain-3 (ch-3) space. Work 3 stitches in the space, then continue to work to the end of the row or to the next chain-3 (ch-3) space.

ONE-STEP BUTTON LOOP

Work to the placement marker of the button loop—single crochet (sc) is shown here. Crochet the desired number of chain (ch) stitches (not too loosely), either don't skip any stitches or skip one or two, then continue to work to the end of the row or to the next marker.

TWO-STEP BUTTON LOOP

These very sturdy loops are perfect for fastening just about any size or shape button, and they add a handsome designer detail as well. Make a test swatch following our general directions (below) to familiarize yourself with this technique.

To make custom-sized loops, simply adjust the amount of chain (ch) stitches and skipped stitches. After you know how many stitches you must skip, you will then be able to measure and mark for their placement.

1. Work in single crochet (sc) for about 10 stitches. Chain (ch) 4 and turn so the wrong side is facing you. Skip 2 stitches, then work 1 slip stitch (sl st) in the next stitch.

2. Chain (ch) 1 and turn so the right side is facing you. Work 6 single crochet (sc) in the loop, or as many single crochet (sc) stitches needed to cover the loop. To continue, single crochet (sc) in the next stitch of the edge.

Buttons can be both a practical and a fun design element, as in this striped cowl. (See page 113 for instructions.)

STRIPES

You can add some color interest to your projects by working in stripes. How you change colors to do this depends on the stitch you are working in, but all the methods are easy enough for even a beginner to master. Let's start with striping **single crochet (sc)**.

A simple stripe pattern elevates a basic silhouette like this elegant jacket. (See page 105 for instructions.)

1. Work across the row to within the last stitch. Insert the hook into the last stitch and draw up a loop. Working 6"/15cm from the end of the new color, draw the new color through both loops on the hook to complete the **single crochet (sc)** stitch.

2. Chain (ch) 1 and turn. Cut the old yarn, leaving a 6"/15cm tail. Loosely tie the two tails together, close to the side edge, so stitches don't unravel. Later, untie the knot and weave in the ends.

For **half double crochet (hdc)**, you'll work to within the last stitch, then yarn over (yo), insert the hook into the last stitch, and draw up the loop. Then draw the new color through all three loops on the hook to complete the stitch. Chain (ch) 2 and turn, then join the yarns as in step 2.

For **double crochet (dc)**, you'll work to within the last stitch, then yarn over (yo), insert the hook into the last stitch, and draw up the loop. Yarn over (yo) again and draw through first 2 loops. Next, draw the new color through the last 2 loops on the hook to complete the stitch. Chain (ch) 3 and turn, then join the yarns as in step 2, above.

For **treble crochet (tr)**, you'll work to within the last stitch. Yarn over (yo) the hook twice and draw through two loops on the hook. Yarn over (yo) again and draw through two loops on the hook. Draw the new color through the last two loops on the hook to complete the stitch. Chain (ch) 4 and turn, then join the yarns as in step 2.

EMBELLISH IT

Here are some fun extras that will give your crochet projects a special touch: pom-poms, fringe, and tassels. The type of yarn you use will affect the look, so take that into consideration when choosing.

POM-POMS

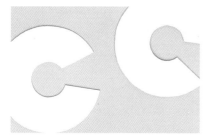

1. With two circular pieces of cardboard the width of the desired pom-pom, cut a center hole. Then cut a pie-shaped wedge out of the circle.

2. Hold the two circles together and wrap the yarn tightly around the cardboard. Carefully cut around the cardboard.

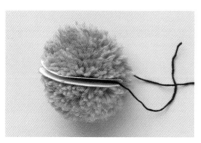

3. Tie a piece of yarn tightly between the two circles. Remove the cardboard and trim the pom-pom.

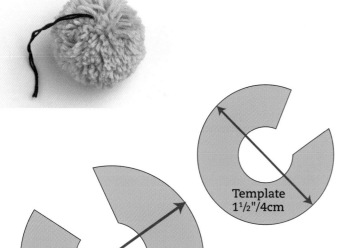

Template 1½"/4cm

Template 2"/5cm

SIMPLE FRINGE

Cut yarn twice the desired length plus extra for knotting. Fold a cluster of strands (between 2 and 4) in half. On the wrong side, insert the hook from front to back through the piece and over the folded yarn. Pull the fold in the yarn through. Draw the ends through the loop and tighten. Trim the yarn.

KNOTTED FRINGE

After working a simple fringe (it should be longer to account for extra knotting), take half of the strands from each fringe and knot them with half the strands from the neighboring fringe.

TASSELS

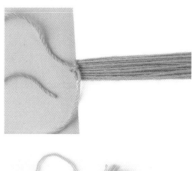

Wrap yarn around cardboard the length of the tassel, leaving a 12"/30cm strand loose at either end. With a yarn needle, knot both sides to the first loop and run the loose strand under the wrapped strands. Pull tightly and tie at the top. Cut the lower edge of the tassel and, holding the tassel about ¾"/2cm from the top, wind the top strands in opposite directions around the tassel. Thread the two strands and insert them through the top of the tassel.

ABBREVIATIONS AND OTHER HELPFUL INFORMATION

At first glance crochet instructions may seem like they are written is some sort of secret code. They're not. It's just that to save space and make directions a bit clearer, those who write patterns have come up with a few shorthand ways to get the point across. The list below should get you through just about any project. We've also included a chart listing the different weights of yarn with gauges and recommended hook sizes.

[ ] or ( )	work directions in brackets or parentheses the number of times indicated	**hdc2tog**	half double crochet 2 sts together
* or **	repeat directions following * or ** as many times as indicated	**inc**	increase(d)/(ing)
		lp(s)	loop(s)
approx	approximately	**m**	meters
beg	begin(ning)	**mm**	millimeters
bet	between	**MC**	main color
bl	back loop	**oz**	ounces
BP	back post	**pat(s)**	pattern(s)
BPdc	back post double crochet	**pm**	place marker
BPsc	back post single crochet	**rem**	remain(ing)
BPtr	back post treble crochet	**rep**	repeat
CC	contrasting color	**rev**	reverse
ch(s)	chain(s)	**rev sc**	reverse single crochet (U.K. rev dc—reverse double crochet)
ch-	refers to chain or space previously made (i.e., ch-1 space)	**rnd(s)**	round(s)
		RS	right side
ch-sp	chain space previously made	**sc**	single crochet (U.K. dc—double crochet)
cl	cluster	**sc2tog**	single crochet 2 sts together
cm	centimeters	**sk**	skip(ped)
dc	double crochet (U.K. tr—treble crochet)	**sl**	slip
dc2tog	double crochet 2 sts together	**sl st**	slip stitch(es) (U.K. sc—single crochet)
dec	decrease(ing)	**sp(s)**	space(s)
dtr	double treble crochet (U.K. trip tr or trtr—triple treble crochet)	**st(s)**	stitch(es)
		t-ch	turning chain
fl	front loop	**tog**	together
foll	follow(s)(ing)	**tr**	treble crochet (U.K. dtr—double treble crochet)
FP	front post		
FPdc	front post double crochet	**trtr**	triple treble (U.K. qtr—quadruple treble crochet)
FPsc	front post single crochet		
FPtr	front post treble crochet	**WS**	wrong side
g	grams	**yo**	yarn over (U.K. yoh—yarn over hook)
grp(s)	group(s)		
hdc	half double crochet (U.K. htr—half treble crochet)		

STANDARD YARN WEIGHT SYSTEM

Categories of yarn, gauge ranges, and recommended needle and hook sizes

Yarn Weight Symbol & Category	0 Lace	1 Super Fine	2 Fine	3 Light	4 Medium	5 Bulky	6 Super Bulky	7 Jumbo
Type of Yarns in Category	Fingering 10-count crochet thread	Sock, Fingering, Baby	Sport, Baby	DK, Light Worsted	Worsted, Afghan, Aran	Chunky, Craft, Rug	Super Bulky, Roving	Jumbo, Roving
Knit Gauge Range* in Stockinette Stitch to 4 inches	33–40** sts	27–32 sts	23–26 sts	21–24 sts	16–20 sts	12–15 sts	7–11 sts	6 sts and fewer
Recommended Needle in Metric Size Range	1.5–2.25 mm	2.25—3.25 mm	3.25—3.75 mm	3.75—4.5 mm	4.5—5.5 mm	5.5—8 mm	8—12.75 mm	12.75 mm and larger
Recommended Needle U.S. Size Range	000–1	1 to 3	3 to 5	5 to 7	7 to 9	9 to 11	11 to 17	17 and larger
Crochet Gauge* Ranges in Single Crochet to 4 inch	32–42 double crochets**	21–32 sts	16–20 sts	12–17 sts	11–14 sts	8–11 sts	6–9 sts	5 sts and fewer
Recommended Hook in Metric Size Range	Steel*** 1.6–1.4 mm	2.25—3.5 mm	3.5—4.5 mm	4.5—5.5 mm	5.5—6.5 mm	6.5—9 mm	9—16 mm	16 mm and larger
Recommended Hook U.S. Size Range	Steel*** 6, 7, 8 Regular hook B–1	B–1 to E–4	E–4 to 7	7 to I–9	I–9 to K–10 1/2	K–10 1/2 to M–13	M–13 to Q	Q and larger

* GUIDELINES ONLY: The above reflect the most commonly used gauges and needle or hook sizes for specific yarn categories.

** Lace weight yarns are usually knitted or crocheted on larger needles and hooks to create lacy, openwork patterns. Accordingly, a gauge range is difficult to determine. Always follow the gauge stated in your pattern.

*** Steel crochet hooks are sized differently from regular hooks—the higher the number, the smaller the hook, which is the reverse of regular hook sizing

TRANSLATION CHART

U.S. Term	U.K./AUS Term
sl st slip stitch	**sc** single crochet
sc single crochet	**dc** double crochet
hdc half double crochet	**htr** half treble crohet
dc double crochet	**tr** treble crochet
tr treble crochet	**dtr** double treble crochet
dtr double treble crochet	**trip tr or trtr** triple treble crochet
trtr triple treble crochet	**qtr** quarduple treble crochet
rev sc reverse single crochet	**rev dc** reverse double crochet
yo yarn over	**yoh** yarn over

SKILL LEVELS

The final section of this book includes more than 25 projects for sweaters, scarves, hats, and more. This key will help you choose a project to fit your skill level.

●

BASIC
Projects using basic stitches. May include basic increases and decreases.

● ●

EASY
Projects may include simple stitch patterns, colorwork, and/or shaping.

● ● ●

INTERMEDIATE
Projects may include involved stitch patterns, colorwork, and/or shaping.

● ● ● ●

COMPLEX
Projects may include complex stitch patterns, colorwork, and/or shaping. using a variety of techniques and stitches.

CROCHET HOOKS

U.S.	METRIC
B/1	2.25mm
C/2	2.75mm
D/3	3.25mm
E/4	3.5mm
F/5	3.75mm
G/6	4mm
7	4.5mm
H/8	5mm
I/9	5.5mm
J/10	6mm
K/10½	6.5mm
L/11	8mm
M/13	9mm
N/15	10mm

UNDERSTANDING CROCHET CHARTS

Every craft has its language, but crochet can also be expressed in symbols. Any crochet pattern—whether it's a motif worked in the round or a flat piece of a stitch pattern—can be represented in a chart. Some crocheters are more visual and prefer to follow charts. Crochet symbols are all quite logical, if you take the time to get to know them. They rise in height along with the stitches they represent—the chain stitch being just a flat oval, the single crochet a squat cross, the half double crochet growing up into a T, and so on—and quite often actually look like the stitches themselves. When the symbols are arranged spatially, the finished chart will, in fact, mimic the work. Following are tips that will help you decipher all those symbols.

MOTIFS

Motif charts (charts for patterns that are worked in the round) start at the center, just like the work does. Each round, marked at its beginning with its round number, builds out from the center; after the initial chain or ring, every odd-numbered round is black and every even-numbered round is a contrasting color (often blue) to help legibility. When the motif is worked without turning between rounds (check your pattern's details), each round is read counterclockwise, mimicking the way the stitches will be worked. (Left-handers who crochet the opposite way can read the rounds clockwise.) Stitches appear in the diagram based on where they should go in the work, but it's not always obvious where to work into a stitch or into a space—oftentimes the written pattern will make this clear, or you can use your own common sense when working the piece. For the most part, though, you'll see how the stitches in each row relate to the ones below: for instance, when two stitches radiate out from one below, you'll know to work both stitches into the one stitch.

JOINING MOTIFS DIAGRAM

MOTIF DIAGRAM

STITCH KEY

•	slip stitch (sl st)		2 double crochet cluster (2 dc-cl)
⚬	chain (ch)		
+	single crochet (sc)		5 double crochet cluster (5 dc-cl)
⊤	double crochet (dc)		
⊤	double treble crochet (dtr)		6 double crochet cluster (6 dc-cl)

Take a look at the motif chart from the Motif Wrap (page 143) shown below. Can you tell how to begin Round 4? It would start: ch 2, 4 dc-cl in same ch of t-ch, *ch 5, 5 dc-cl in next dtr, and it would repeat from there. The round would end with ch 2, dc in 4 dc-cl. When a pattern is made up of many motifs that are joined as you go, the diagram will show one complete motif, which refers to the motif you are currently working, and a shadow of a second, partial motif, which is the motif to which you are joining. It will also show joining areas, and you can use this information for all subsequent joinings.

STITCH PATTERNS

Stitch patterns as well as partial motifs are worked back and forth instead of in the round, so the diagrams are read this way as well. They are often condensed versions of the entire pattern, showing just a part or highlighting the pattern repeat. The written pattern will specify how many stitches are in the initial chain, which can be read on the diagram from left to right.

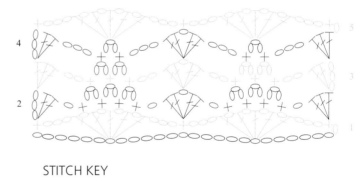

STITCH KEY

◯ chain (ch)   + single crochet (sc)   ⊤ double crochet (tr)

Start reading Row 1 from right to left—exactly how you work down your foundation chain. The stitch pattern begins at the bottom and builds up, with the stitches lining up from row to row. Here again the rows alternate between black and blue to help you differentiate them. The placement of the row number represents the beginning of the row and therefore the direction in which you read the chart. The lace stitch pattern from the Shell-Stitch Cowl (page 94) is shown above. As you can see, the written pattern and the stitch diagram work hand in hand to give you a complete picture.

STITCH
DICTIONARY

Now that you've got the basics down,
try your hand at dozens of beautiful stitch patterns:
classic stitches, geometric motifs,
vibrant colorwork, delicate lace, versatile
edgings, and more.

SINGLE CROCHET CHAIN 1

(ch a multiple of 2 sts + 2)

Row 1 Work 1 sc in 2nd ch from hook, *ch 1, skip next ch, sc in next ch; rep from * to end. Turn.

Row 2 Ch 1, 1 sc in first sc, *1 sc in next ch-1 sp, ch 1; rep from * to last ch-1 sp, 1 sc in ch-1 sp, 1 sc in last sc. Turn.

Row 3 Ch 1, 1 sc in first sc, *ch 1, 1 sc in next ch-1 sp; rep from * to last 2 sc, ch 1, skip next sc, 1 sc in last sc. Turn.

Rep rows 2 and 3.

BACK LOOP SINGLE CROCHET

(ch any multiple of sts + 1)

Row 1 Work 1 sc in 2nd ch from hook and in each ch across. Turn.

Row 2 Ch 1, working in back lps only, 1 sc in each sc across. Turn.

Rep row 2.

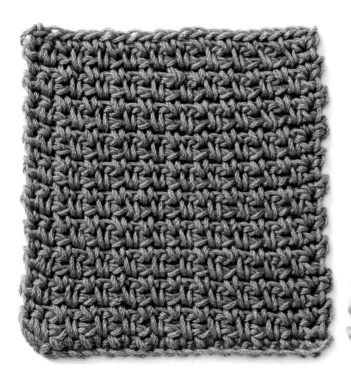

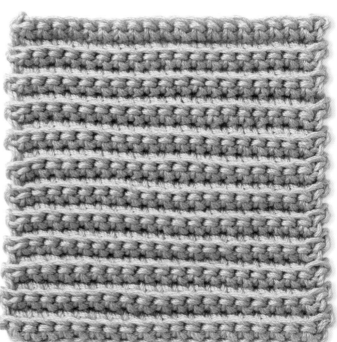

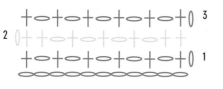

Stitch Key

⬭ chain (ch)

† single crochet (sc)

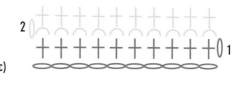

Stitch Key

⬭ chain (ch)

† single crochet (sc)

⟂ single crochet through back loop (sc tbl)

HALF DOUBLE CROCHET

(ch any multiple of sts + 2)

Row 1 Work 1 hdc in 3rd ch from hook and in each ch across. Turn.

Row 2 Ch 2, 1 hdc in each hdc across. Turn.

Rep row 2.

SOLID SCALLOP

(ch a multiple of 6 sts + 2)

Row 1 Work 1 sc in 2nd ch from hook, *skip 2 ch, 5 dc in next ch, skip 2 ch, 1 sc in next ch; rep from * across. Turn.

Row 2 Ch 3 (counts as 1 dc), 2 dc in first sc, *1 sc in center dc of next scallop, 5 dc in next sc; rep from *, end last rep 3 dc in last sc. Turn.

Row 3 Ch 1, 1 sc in first dc, *5 dc in next sc, 1 sc in center dc of next scallop; rep from *, end last rep 1 sc in top of t-ch. Turn.

Rep rows 2 and 3.

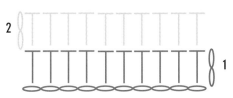

Stitch Key

⬭ chain (ch)

┬ half double crochet (hdc)

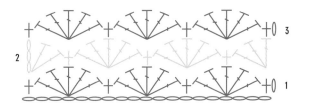

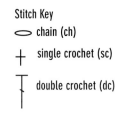

Stitch Key

⬭ chain (ch)

+ single crochet (sc)

┬ double crochet (dc)

WIDE RIB

(ch any multiple of sts + 3)

Row 1 Work 1 dc in 4th ch from hook and in each ch across. Turn.

Row 2 Working through both lps across row, 1 sc in first st, insert hook in same st and draw up a lp, insert hook in next st and draw up a lp, draw last lp directly through 2 lps on hook, *insert hook in same st as last completed st, yo and draw up a lp, insert hook in next st and draw up a lp, draw last lp directly through 2 lps on hook; rep from * in each st across, work additional sl st in last st. Turn.

Row 3 Ch 3, working in back lps only, 1 dc in each st across. Turn.

Rep rows 2 and 3.

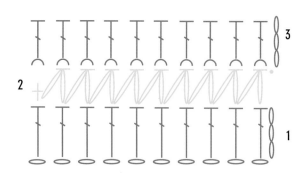

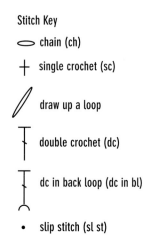

Stitch Key

⬭ chain (ch)

✛ single crochet (sc)

╱ draw up a loop

┬ double crochet (dc)

┬ dc in back loop (dc in bl)

⌒ slip stitch (sl st)

WAVE PATTERN

(ch a multiple of 12 sts + 5)

Row 1 In 6th ch from hook work [1 tr, ch 1] 3 times, skip 5 ch, 1 sc in next ch, *ch 1, skip 5 ch, in next ch work [1 tr, ch 1] 7 times, skip 5 ch, 1 sc in next ch; rep from * to last 6 ch, ch 1, in last ch work [1 tr, ch 1] 3 times, 1 tr in same ch. Turn.

Row 2 Ch 1, 1 sc in first tr, *ch 6, 1 sc in next sc, ch 6, skip 3 tr, 1 sc in next tr; rep from *, end last rep 1 sc in 4th ch of t-ch. Turn.

Row 3 Ch 1, 1 sc in first sc, *ch 6, 1 sc in next sc; rep from * across. Turn.

Row 4 Ch 1, 1 sc in first sc, *ch 1, in next sc work [1 tr, ch 1] 7 times, 1 sc in next sc; rep from * across. Turn.

Row 5 Ch 1, 1 sc in first sc, *ch 6, skip 3 tr, 1 sc in next tr, ch 6, 1 sc in next sc; rep from * across. Turn.

Row 6 Rep row 3.

Row 7 Ch 5 (counts as 1 tr and ch 1), in first sc work [1 tr, ch 1] 3 times, 1 sc in next sc, *ch 1, in next sc work [1 tr, ch 1] 7 times, 1 sc in next sc; rep from * to last sc, in last sc work [ch 1, 1 tr] 4 times. Turn.

Rep rows 2–7.

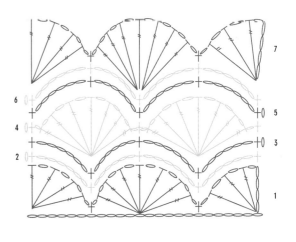

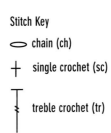

Stitch Key

⬭ chain (ch)

✛ single crochet (sc)

⊤ treble crochet (tr)

PETITE POPCORNS

(ch a multiple of 3 sts + 2)

Row 1 Work 1 sc in 2nd ch from hook and in each ch across. Turn.

Row 2 Ch 1, 1 sc in first sc, *in next sc [yo and draw up a lp] 5 times, yo and draw through all 5 lps on hook (Popcorn made), 1 sc in each of next 2 sc; rep from * across. Turn.

Row 3 Ch 1, 1 sc in each st across. Turn.

Row 4 Ch 1, *1 sc in next 2 sc, Popcorn in next sc; rep from *, end 1 sc in last sc. Turn.

Row 5 Rep row 3.

Rep rows 2–5.

CROCHET CABLE

(ch a multiple of 4 sts + 3)

Row 1 Work 1 sc in 2nd ch from hook and in each ch across. Turn.

Row 2 Ch 3 (counts as 1 dc), *skip next sc, 1 dc in next 3 sc, yo, with hook in front of work, go *back* and insert hook from *front* to *back* into skipped st before the 3-dc group; loosely draw through a lp and bring it up to the height of the 3-dc group; yo and complete dc (Cable st); rep from * across, end dc in last st. Turn.

Row 3 Ch 1, 1 sc in each dc across. Turn.

Rep rows 2 and 3.

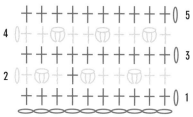

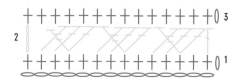

Stitch Key

⬯ chain (ch)

✛ single crochet (sc)

⬭ popcorn

Stitch Key

⬯ chain (ch)

✛ single crochet (sc)

┬ double crochet (dc)

ALTERNATING RIDGE PATTERN

(ch a multiple of 2 sts + 1)

Row 1 Work 1 sc in 2nd ch from hook, *skip next ch, 2 sc in next ch; rep from *, end 1 sc in last ch. Turn.

Row 2 Ch 2, hdc in first st, *skip next st, 2 hdc in next st; rep from *, end hdc in last st. Turn.

Row 3 Ch 1, 1 sc in first st, *skip next st, 2 sc in next st; rep from *, end sc in last st. Turn.

Row 4 Rep row 3.

Rep rows 2–4.

FRONT LOOP DOUBLE CROCHET

(ch any multiple of sts + 3)

Row 1 Work 1 dc in 4th ch from hook and in each ch across. Turn.

Row 2 Ch 3 (counts as 1 dc), skip first dc, working through front lps only, 1 dc in each st across, dc in top of t-ch. Turn.

Rep row 2.

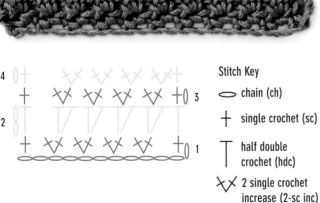

Stitch Key

- ◯ chain (ch)
- ✛ single crochet (sc)
- ⊤ half double crochet (hdc)
- ✕✕ 2 single crochet increase (2-sc inc)

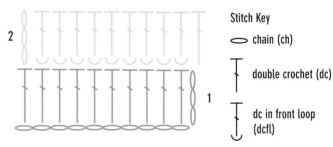

Stitch Key

- ◯ chain (ch)
- ⊤ double crochet (dc)
- ↧ dc in front loop (dcfl)

WAVY RIB

FPdc Yo, insert hook from front to back to front around post of next st of row below, yo and draw up a lp, [yo and draw through 2 lps on hook] twice.

BPdc Yo, insert hook from back to front to back around post of next st of row below, yo and draw up a lp, [yo and draw through 2 lps on hook] twice.

(ch a multiple of 2 sts + 3)
Foundation row Dc in 4th ch from hook and in each ch across. Turn.
Row 1 Ch 3 (counts as 1 dc), skip first dc, *1 FPdc around next st of row below, 1 dc in next st; rep from * to last st, 1 FPdc around next st of row below, 1 dc in top of t-ch. Turn.
Row 2 Ch 3 (counts as 1 dc), skip first dc, *1 BPdc around next st of row below, 1 dc in next dc; rep from * to last st, 1 BPdc around next st of row below, 1 dc in top of t-ch. Turn.
Rep rows 1 and 2.

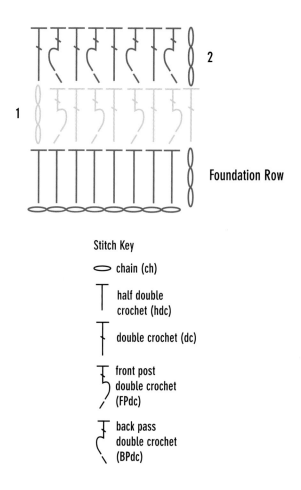

Foundation Row

Stitch Key

⬯ chain (ch)

┬ half double
crochet (hdc)

┬ double crochet (dc)

front post
double crochet
(FPdc)

back pass
double crochet
(BPdc)

PRETTY BALLERINA

(colors A, B, C, and D)

(with A, ch 4 and join with sl st in first ch to form ring)

Rnd 1 [1 sc, ch 3] 4 times in ring. Join with sl st to first sc.

Rnd 2 Sl st in ch-3 sp, ch 3 (counts as 1 dc), (2 dc, ch 3, 3 dc) in same sp, *[(3 dc, ch 3, 3 dc) in next sp] 3 times. Join with sl st to top of beg ch-3—4 corner ch-3 sps. Fasten off.

Rnd 3 With B and lp on hook, (1 sc, ch 3, 1 sc) in corner ch-3 sp, *ch 3, 1 sc between next 3rd and 4th dc, ch 3, (1 sc, ch 3, 1 sc) in next corner ch-3 sp; rep from *, end ch 3, 1 sc between next 3rd and 4th dc, ch 3. Join with sl st to first sc.

Rnd 4 Sl st in corner ch-3 sp, ch 3 (counts as 1 dc), (2 dc, ch 3, 3 dc) in same corner, *[3 dc in next ch-3 sp] twice**, (3 dc, ch 3, 3 dc) in next corner; rep from * twice more, then from * to ** once. Join with sl st to top of beg ch-3. Fasten off.

Rnd 5 With C and lp on hook, *(1 sc, ch 3, 1 sc) in corner ch-3 sp, [ch 3, 1 sc between next 3rd and 4th dc] 3 times, ch 3; rep from * to around. Join with sl st to first sc.

Rnd 6 Sl st in corner ch-3 sp, ch 3 (counts as 1 dc), (2 dc, ch 3, 3 dc) in same corner, *[3 dc in next ch-3 sp] 4 times**, (3 dc, ch 3, 3 dc) in next corner; rep from * twice more, then from * to ** once. Join with sl st to top of beg ch-3. Fasten off.

Rnd 7 With D and lp on hook, (1 sc, ch 7, 1 sc) in corner ch-3 sp, [ch 5, 1 sc between next 3rd and 4th dc] 5 times, *ch 5, (1 sc, ch 7, 1 sc) in next corner ch-3 sp, [ch 5, 1 sc between next 3rd and 4th dc] 5 times; rep from *, end ch 5. Join with sl st to first sc. Fasten off.

Color Key

- A
- B
- C
- D

Stitch Key

 chain (ch)

single crochet (sc)

double crochet (dc)

• slip stitch (sl st)

47

RADIANT

CL2 (dc2tog) [Yo and insert hook into st, yo and draw up a lp through st, yo and draw through 2 lps on hook] twice, yo and draw through all 3 lps on hook.

CL3 (dc3tog) [Yo and insert hook into st, yo and draw up a lp through st, yo and draw through 2 lps on hook] 3 times, yo and draw through all 4 lps on hook.

(colors A, B, and C)

(with A, ch 5 and join with sl st in first ch to form ring)

Rnd 1 Ch 3, CL2, [ch 3, CL3] 7 times in ring, end ch 3. Join with sl st to top of first cluster—8 clusters. Fasten off.

Rnd 2 With B, sl st in first corner ch-3 sp, ch 3 (counts as 1 dc), (2 dc, ch 3, 3 dc) in same ch-3 sp, *3 hdc in next ch-3 sp, (3 dc, ch 3, 3 dc) in corner ch-3 sp; rep from *, end 3 hdc in last ch-3 sp. Join with sl st to top of beg ch-3 changing to A. Fasten off.

Rnd 3 With A, sl st in same place as joining, ch 1, 1 sc in next 2 sts, *(2 sc, ch 2, 2 sc) in next corner ch-3 sp, skip 1 dc, 1 sc in next 8 sts; rep from *, end last rep 1 sc in last 6 sts. Join with sl st to first sc. Fasten off.

Rnd 4 With B and lp on hook, 1 sc in first ch-2 sp, 1 sc in same sp, *1 sc in 12 sc, 2 sc in corner ch-2 sp; rep from * around. Join with sl st to first sc. Fasten off.

Rnd 5 With C and lp on hook, 2 sc in first st of first corner, 2 sc in next corner st of same corner, *1 sc in next 12 sc [2 sc in next corner sc] twice; rep from * around, end 1 sc in last 12 sc. Join with sl st to first sc. Fasten off.

Color Key

- A
- B
- C

Stitch Key

⌒ chain (ch)

+ single crochet (sc)

| half double crochet (hdc)

⊤ double crochet (dc)

• slip stitch (sl st)

⋀ double crochet 2 tog (CL2)

⋀ double crochet 3 tog (CL3)

WAGON WHEEL

CL (3-hdc Puff) [Yo and draw up a lp] 3 times in same sp, yo and draw through all 7 lps on hook.

(ch 5 and join with sl st in first ch to form ring)
Rnd 1 (RS) Ch 5 (counts as 1 tr and ch 1), [1 tr, ch 1] 11 times in ring. Join with sl st in 4th ch of beg ch-5—12 tr.
Rnd 2 [CL, ch 1] twice in first ch-1 sp, *[CL, ch 1] twice in next ch-1 sp; rep from * around. Join with sl st to top of first puff st—24 puff sts.
Rnd 3 Sl st in first ch-1 sp, ch 6 (counts as 1 tr and ch 2), 1 tr in same sp—first corner, *ch 1, 1 dc in next ch-1 sp, [ch 1, 1 hdc in next ch-1 sp] 3 times, ch 1, 1 dc in next ch-1 sp, ch 1**, (1 tr, ch 2, 1 tr) in next corner ch-1 sp; rep from * twice more, then from * to ** once. Join with sl st in 4th ch of beg ch-6. Fasten off.

Stitch Key

⬯ chain (ch)

+ single crochet (sc)

T half double crochet (hdc)

† double crochet (dc)

‡ treble crochet (tr)

• slip stitch (sl st)

◊ 3 - half double crochet puff (CL)

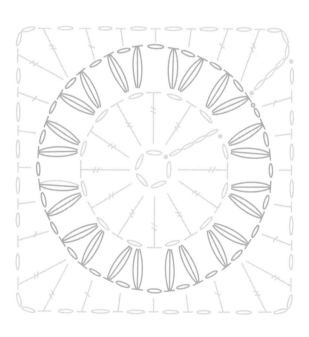

PINWHEEL

CL3 (3-st Puff) [Yo and draw up a lp, yo and draw through 1 lp on hook] 3 times in same sp, yo and through all 7 lps.
CL4 (4-st Puff) [Yo and draw up a lp, yo and draw through 1 lp on hook] 4 times in same sp, yo and through all 9 lps.

(ch 6 and join with sl st in first ch to form ring)
Rnd 1 Ch 4 (counts as 1 dc and ch 1), [1 dc, ch 1] 11 times in ring—12 ch-1 sps. Join with sl st in 3rd ch of beg ch-4.
Rnd 2 Sl st into first ch-1 sp, (ch 3, CL3) in same sp, ch 2, *CL4 in next ch-1 sp, (ch 3, 1 tr in dc, ch 3) for corner, [CL4 in ch-1 sp, ch 2] twice; rep from *, end last rep CL4 in ch-1 sp, ch 2. Join with sl st to top of first puff st.
Rnd 3 Ch 1, 1 sc in same place as joining, *ch 2, skip next ch-2 sp, 4 dc in next ch-3 sp, ch 2, 1 tr in tr, [ch 3, insert hook down through top of last tr and sl st]—(Picot), ch 2, 4 dc in next ch-3 sp, ch 2, skip next ch-2 sp, 1 sc in CL4; rep from *, end last rep 4 dc in last ch-3 sp, ch 2, skip last ch-2 sp. Join with sl st to first sc. Fasten off.

Stitch Key

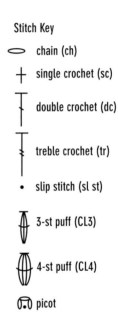

chain (ch)

single crochet (sc)

double crochet (dc)

treble crochet (tr)

slip stitch (sl st)

3-st puff (CL3)

4-st puff (CL4)

picot

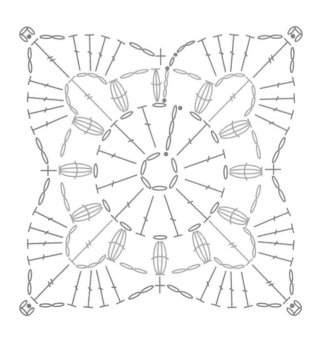

TILTED CLUSTER

CL2 (2-dc Cluster) [Yo and draw up a lp, yo and draw through 2 lps on hook] twice in same sp, yo and draw through all 3 lps on hook.

CL3 (3-dc Cluster) [Yo and draw up a lp, yo and draw through 2 lps on hook] 3 times in same sp, yo and draw through all 4 lps on hook.

(colors A, B, and C)

(with A, ch 4 and join with sl st in first ch to form ring)

Rnd 1 Ch 4 (counts as 1 dc and ch 1), [1 dc, ch 1] 11 times in ring. Join with sl st to 3rd ch of beg ch-4 —12 ch-1 sps. Fasten off.

Rnd 2 With B, sl st to a ch-1 sp, (ch 3, CL2) in same ch-1 sp, [ch 3, CL3 in next ch-1 sp] 11 times, ch 3. Join with sl st to top of CL2— 12 clusters. Fasten off.

Rnd 3 With C and lp on hook, 1 sc in ch-3 sp, ch 5, [1 sc in ch-3 sp, ch 5] 11 times. Join with sl st to first sc. Fasten off.

Rnd 4 With B, 1 sc in first ch-5 sp, *ch 5, 1 sc in next ch-5 sp, ch 1, (5 dc, ch 3, 5 dc) in next ch-5 sp, ch 1**, 1 sc in next ch-5 sp; rep from * twice more, then from * to ** once. Join with sl st to first sc. Fasten off.

Color Key

 A

B

C

Stitch Key

⬯ chain (ch)

+ single crochet (sc)

↑ double crochet (dc)

• slip stitch (sl st)

2-double crochet cluster (CL2)

3-double crochet cluster (CL3)

STAR PUFF

CL2 (2-st Puff) [Yo and draw up a lp, yo and draw through 1 lp on hook] twice in same sp, yo and draw through all 5 lps on hook.
CL3 (3-st Puff) [Yo and draw up a lp, yo and draw through 1 lp on hook] 3 times in same sp, yo and draw through all 7 lps on hook.

(colors A and B)
(with A, ch 7 and join with sl st in first ch to form ring)
Rnd 1 Ch 1, 12 sc in ring. Join with sl st to first sc.
Rnd 2 Ch 3 (counts as 1 dc), 1 dc in next sc, [ch 3, 1 dc in next 2 sc] 5 times, ch 3. Join with sl st to top of beg ch-3—6 ch-3 sps. Fasten off.
Rnd 3 With B, sl st in first ch-3 sp, ch 3 (counts as 1 dc), (CL2, ch 4, CL3) in same ch-3 sp, [ch 4, (CL3, ch 4, CL3) in next ch-3 sp] 5 times, ch 4. Join with sl st to top of CL2.
Rnd 4 Ch 1, (2 sc, ch 4, 2 sc) in first ch-4 sp, [(2 sc, ch 4, 2 sc) in next ch-4 sp] 11 times. Join with sl st to first sc. Fasten off.

Color Key

□ A

■ B

Stitch Key

⬭ chain (ch)

+ single crochet (sc)

T double crochet (dc)

• slip stitch (sl st)

Ⅱ 2-double crochet cluster (CL2)

Ⅲ 3-double crochet cluster (CL3)

HALF STAR

CL2 (2-st Puff) [Yo and draw up a lp, yo and draw through 1 lp on hook] twice, yo and draw through all 5 lps on hook.
CL3 (3-st Puff) [Yo and draw up a lp, yo and draw through 1 lp on hook] 3 times, yo and draw through all 7 lps on hook.

(colors A and B)
(with A, ch 7 and join with sl st in first ch to form ring)
Row 1 (WS) Ch 1, 8 sc in ring. Do not join. Turn.
Row 2 (RS) Ch 4 (counts as 1 dc and ch 1), skip first sc, [1 dc in 2 sc, ch 3] twice, 1 dc in next 2 sc, ch 1, 1 dc in last sc. Fasten off.
Row 3 (RS) With B and lp on hook, (1 sc, ch 3, CL2) in first ch-1 sp, [ch 4, (CL3, ch 4, CL3) in next ch-3 sp] twice, ch 4, (CL3, ch 1, 1 dc) in last ch-1 sp.
Row 4 (RS) With B and lp on hook, (1 sc, ch 3, 2 sc) in first ch-3 sp at beg of row 3, *(2 sc, ch 3, 2 sc) in next ch-4 sp; rep from * 4 times more, end (2 sc, ch 3, 1 sc) in last ch-1 sp. Fasten off.

Color Key
■ A
■ B

Stitch Key
⬯ chain (ch)

+ single crochet (sc)

T double crochet (dc)

• slip stitch (sl st)

2-double crochet cluster (CL2)

3-double crochet cluster (CL3)

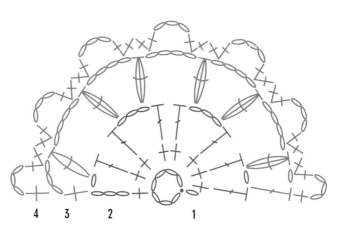

4 3 2 1

HELIANTHUS

(colors A and B)

(with A, ch 6 and join with sl st in first ch to form ring)

Rnd 1 Ch 3 (counts as 1 dc), 15 dc in ring. Join with sl st to top of beg ch-3—16 dc. Fasten off.

Rnd 2 With B, sl st in top of joining, ch 5 (counts as 1 dc and ch 2), 1 dc in same place as joining, [ch 1, skip 1 dc, (1 dc, ch 2, 1 dc) in next dc] 7 times, end ch 1. Join with sl st in 3rd ch of beg ch-5.

Rnd 3 Sl st in first ch-2 sp, ch 3 (counts as 1 dc), (1 dc, ch 2, 2 dc) in same ch-2 sp, *ch 1, (2 dc, ch 2, 2 dc) in next ch-2 sp; rep from * around, ch 1. Join with sl st to top of beg ch-3.

Rnd 4 Sl st in next dc and first ch-2 sp, ch 4 (counts as 1 tr), 7 tr in same ch-2 sp, *1 sc in ch-1 sp, 8 tr in ch-2 sp; rep from * around. Join by inserting hook through ch-1 sp, then 1 sc in 4th ch of beg ch-4. Fasten off.

Color Key

■ A

□ B

Stitch Key

⬯ chain (ch)

+ single crochet (sc)

┬ double crochet (dc)

⌡ treble crochet (tr)

• slip stitch (sl st)

FLAX FLOWER

(colors A, B, and C)

(with A, ch 5 and join with sl st in first ch to form ring)

Rnd 1 Ch 3 (counts as 1 hdc and ch 1), [1 hdc in ring, ch 1] 11 times. Join with sl st in 2nd ch of beg ch-3, changing to B—12 ch-1 sps. Fasten off A.

Rnd 2 With B, ch 2 (counts as 1 hdc), 1 hdc in first ch-1 sp, *ch 1, 2 hdc in next ch-1 sp; rep from * around, ch 1. Join with sl st to top of beg ch-2. Fasten off.

Rnd 3 With C and lp on hook, (1 sc, 2 hdc, 1 sc) in each ch-1 sp around. Join with sl st to first sc. Fasten off.

Color Key

- A
- B
- C

Stitch Key

 chain (ch)

single crochet (sc)

half double crochet (hdc)

• slip stitch (sl st)

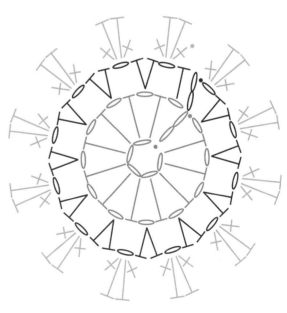

MAY FLOWER

(ch 8 and join with sl st in first ch to form ring)

Rnd 1 Ch 1, 16 sc in ring. Join with sl st to first sc.

Rnd 2 Ch 5 (counts as 1 dc and ch 2), *skip 1 sc, 1 dc in next sc, ch 2; rep from * around, skip 1 sc. Join with sl st in 3rd ch of beg ch-5—8 ch-2 sps.

Rnd 3 Sl st in ch-2 sp, ch 1, (1 sc, 1 hdc, 1 dc, 1 hdc, 1 sc) in each ch-2 sp around. Join with sl st to first sc—8 petals.

Rnd 4 Sl st to first dc, ch 1, sc in same st as last sl st, [ch 4, skip 4 sts, 1 sc in next dc] 7 times, ch 4. Join with sl st to first sc.

Rnd 5 Sl st in first ch-4 sp, ch 1, (1 sc, 1 hdc, 3 dc, 1 hdc, 1 sc) each ch-4 sp around. Join with sl st to first sc. Fasten off.

Stitch Key

⬭	chain (ch)
✚	single crochet (sc)
⊤	half double crochet (hdc)
⊤	double crochet (dc)
•	slip stitch (sl st)

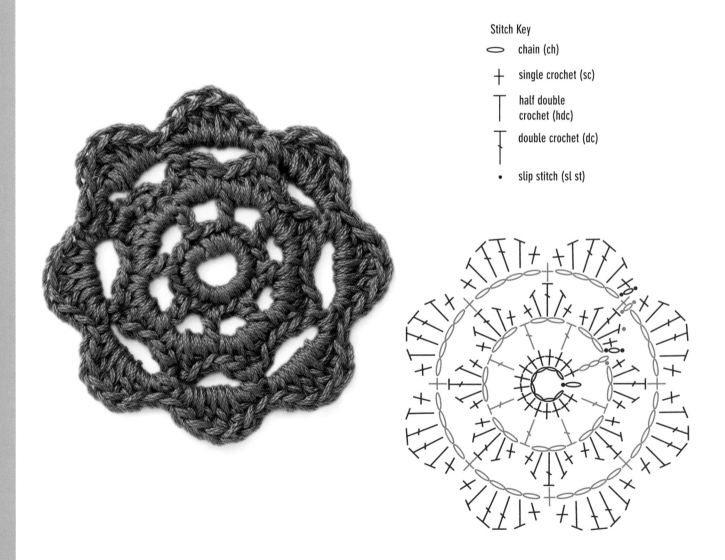

MIRABILIS

Picot (3-ch) Ch 3, sl st in 3rd ch from hook.

(ch 7 and join with sl st in first ch to form ring)

Rnd 1 Ch 1 (counts as 1 sc throughout), 23 sc in ring. Join with sl st to beg ch-1—24 sc.

Rnd 2 Ch 1, 1 sc in each sc around. Join with sl st to beg ch-1.

Rnd 3 Ch 1, 1 sc in first sc, *Picot, 1 sc in 2 sc; rep from * around, end Picot. Join with sl st to beg ch-1.

Rnd 4 Ch 8 (counts as 1 dtr and ch 4), *skip Picot, 1 dtr in next sc, ch 4; rep from * around. Join with sl st in 4th ch of beg ch-8.

Rnd 5 8 Sc in each ch-4 sp around. Join with sl st to first sc.

Rnd 6 Sl st to first sc, ch 1, 1 sc in next 5 sc, skip 1 sc, *[1 sc in next 2 sc, Picot] 3 times, 1 sc in 2 sc, skip 1 sc, 1 sc in next 6 sc, skip 1 sc; rep from * around, end [1 sc in next 2 sc, Picot] 3 times, 1 sc in last 2 sc. Join with sl st to beg ch-1. Fasten off.

Stitch Key

⌒ chain (ch)

+ single crochet (sc)

𝑇 double treble crochet (dtr)

• slip stitch (sl st)

picot (3-ch)

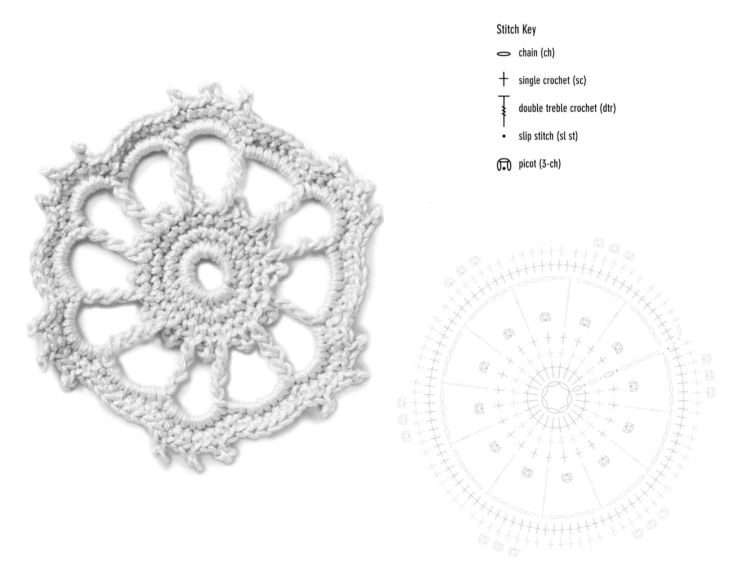

NARCISSUS

BPdc (Back Post dc) Yo, insert hook from back to front to back around post of st directly below and draw up a lp, complete as dc.

(colors A, B, and C)

(with A, ch 5, and join with sl st to form ring)

Rnd 1 Ch 4 (counts as 1 dc and ch 1), [1 dc in ring, ch 1] 11 times. Join with sl st in 2nd ch of beg ch-3—12 ch-1 sps. Fasten off.

Rnd 2 With B and lp on hook, (1 sc, 1 hdc, 1 sc) in each ch-1 sp around. Join with sl st in top of first sc. Fasten off.

Rnd 3 With A and lp on hook, insert hook from back to front to back around post of dc from rnd 1 and make a sl st, BPdc around post of same st as sl st, ch 2, *BPdc around next dc from rnd 1, ch 2; rep from * around. Join with sl st in top of first st. Fasten off.

Rnd 4 With C, sl st in first ch-2 sp, ch 2 (counts as 1 hdc), 2 hdc in same ch-2 sp as joining, 3 hdc in each rem ch-2 sp around. Join with sl st to top of beg ch-2. Fasten off.

Color Key

 A

B

C

Stitch Key

⌔ chain (ch)

✛ single crochet (sc)

T half double crochet (hdc)

• slip stitch (sl st)

ʃ back post double crochet (BPdc)

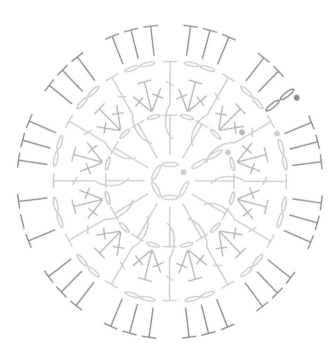

OXALIS

Spike sc Insert hook 2 rnds below (or into first rnd), yo and draw up a lp in this sp to the height of the edge being worked on, yo and draw through both lps on hook.
Picot (3-ch) Ch 3, sl st in 3rd ch from hook.

(colors A and B)
(with A, ch 8 and join with sl st to form ring)
Rnd 1 Ch 1, 16 sc in ring. Join with sl st to first sc, changing to B. Fasten off A.
Rnd 2 With B, (ch 1, 1 sc) in same st as joining, 1 sc in next sc, *(1 sc, ch 7, 1 sc) in next sc, 1 sc in next 3 sc; rep from *, end last rep 1 sc in last sc. Join with sl st to first sc.
Rnd 3 Ch 1, 1 sc in same st as joining, *skip 2 sc, (2 hdc, 15 dc, 2 hdc) into next ch-7 lp, skip 2 sc, 1 sc in next sc; rep from *, end last rep omitting 1 sc in next sc. Join with sl st to first sc. Fasten off.
Rnd 4 With A, sl st to first sc of rnd 3, Spike sc in first sc of rnd 1, *[ch 4, skip next 4 sts of rnd 3, 1 sc in next st, Picot] 3 times, ch 4, skip 4 sts**, Spike sc in next sc of rnd 1; rep from * twice more, then from * to ** once. Join with sl st to top of beg Spike sc. Fasten off.

Color Key

▨ A

▨ B

Stitch Key

⬭ chain (ch)

+ single crochet (sc)

T half double crochet (hdc)

Ŧ double crochet (dc)

• slip stitch (sl st)

⊙ picot

SKINNY STRIPES

(colors A and B)
Stripe Sequence 6 rows A, 1B

(ch any multiple of sts + 1)
Row 1 (RS) With A, 1 sc in 2nd ch from hook and in each ch across. Turn.
Rows 2–6 With A, ch 1, 1 sc in first and in each sc across. Turn.
Row 7 With B, rep row 2.
Row 8 With A, rep row 2.
Rep rows 2–8.

WIDE STRIPES

(colors A and B)
Stripe Sequence 3 rows A, 3B

(ch any multiple of sts + 3)
Row 1 With A, 1 dc in 4th ch from hook and in each ch across. Turn.
Rows 2 and 3 With A, ch 3 (counts as 1 dc throughout), skip first st, 1 dc in next and each dc across, end dc in top of t-ch. Turn.
Rows 4–6 With B, rep row 2.
Row 7 With A, rep row 2.
Rep rows 2–7.

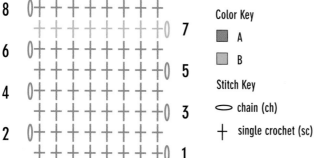

Color Key
■ A
□ B

Stitch Key
⬯ chain (ch)
+ single crochet (sc)

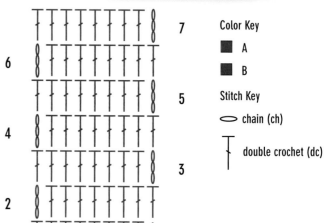

Color Key
■ A
■ B

Stitch Key
⬯ chain (ch)
⊤ double crochet (dc)

STRIPED CHEVRON

(colors A, B, and C)
Stripe Sequence 2 rows A, 2B, 2C

(ch a multiple of 10 sts + 1)
Row 1 Work 2 sc in 2nd ch from hook, *1 sc in next 3 ch, skip 1 ch, 1 sc in next ch, skip 1 ch, 1 sc in next 3 ch, 3 sc in next ch; rep from * to last 10 ch, 1 sc in next 3 ch, skip 1 ch, 1 sc in next ch, skip 1 ch, 1 sc in next 3 ch, 2 sc in last ch. Turn.
Row 2 Ch 1, 2 sc in first sc, *1 sc in next 3 sc, skip 1 sc, 1 sc in next sc, skip 1 sc, 1 sc in next 3 sc, 3 sc in next sc; rep from * to last 10 sc, 1 sc in next 3 sc, skip 1 sc, 1 sc in next sc, skip 1 sc, 1 sc in next 3 sc, 2 sc in last sc. Turn.
Rep row 2, continuing stripe sequence.

JAGGED STRIPES

(colors A and B)
Stripe Sequence 2 rows A, 2B

(ch a multiple of 2 sts)
Row 1 With A, 1 sc in 2nd ch from hook, *ch 1, skip 1 ch, 1 sc in next ch; rep from * to end. Turn.
Row 2 With A, ch 1, 1 sc in first sc, *1 sc in ch-1 sp, ch 1, skip 1 sc; rep from *, end 1 sc in last ch-1 sp, 1 sc in last sc. Turn.
Row 3 With B, ch 1, 1 sc in first sc, *ch 1, skip next sc, 1 sc in next ch-1 sp; rep from *, end ch 1, skip next sc, 1 sc in last sc. Turn.
Row 4 With B, rep row 2.
Row 5 With A, rep row 3.
Row 6 Rep row 2.
Rep rows 3–6.

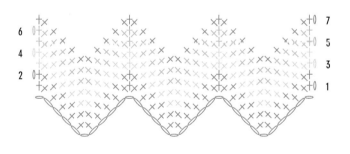

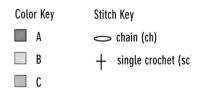

Color Key
- ⬛ A
- ⬜ B
- ⬜ C

Stitch Key
- ⬯ chain (ch)
- ＋ single crochet (sc)

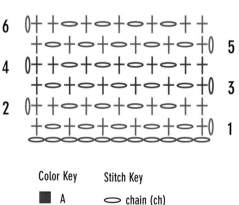

Color Key
- ⬛ A
- ⬛ B

Stitch Key
- ⬯ chain (ch)
- ＋ single crochet (sc)

61

SCALLOP STRIPES

(colors A, B, and C)

Stripe Sequence 2 rows A, 2B, 2C, 2B, 2A, 2C

(ch a multiple of 11 sts + 10)

Row 1 Work 1 dc in 4th ch from hook, ch 1, skip 2 ch, 1 sc in next ch, *ch 5, skip 4 ch, 1 sc in next ch, ch 1, skip 2 ch, (1 dc, ch 1, 1 dc) in next ch, ch 1, skip 2 ch, 1 sc in next ch; rep from *, end ch 2, skip 2 ch, 1 dc in last ch. Turn.

Row 2 Ch 1, 1 sc in first dc, skip ch-2 sp, *3 dc in each of next 3 ch-1 sps, 1 sc in next ch-5 sp; rep from *, end 3 dc in last ch-1 sp, 2 dc in top of t-ch. Turn.

Row 3 Ch 4, 1 sc between 2nd and 3rd dc of first scallop, *ch 1, (1 dc, ch 1, 1 dc) in next sc, ch 1, 1 sc between first and 2nd dc of next scallop, ch 5, skip next scallop, 1 sc between 2nd and 3rd dc of next scallop; rep from *, end ch 1, 2 dc in last sc. Turn.

Row 4 Ch 3, 1 dc in first dc, 3 dc in ch-1 sp, *1 sc in ch-5 sp, 3 dc in next 3 ch-1 sps; rep from *, end 1 sc in t-ch sp. Turn.

Row 5 Ch 3, 1 dc in first sc, ch 1, *1 sc between first and 2nd dc of next scallop, ch 5, skip next scallop, 1 sc between between 2nd and 3rd dc of next scallop, ch 1, (1 dc, ch 1, 1 dc) in next sc, ch 1; rep from *, end 1 sc between first and 2nd dc of last scallop, ch 2, 1 dc in top of t-ch. Turn.

Rep rows 2–5, continuing stripe sequence.

Color Key

■ A
■ B
■ C

Stitch Key

⬭ chain (ch)

+ single crochet (sc)

T double crochet (dc)

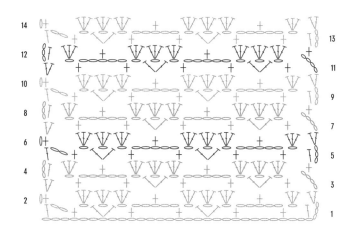

RAINBOW CHEVRON

Sc2tog [Insert hook in next st, yo and draw up a lp] twice, yo and draw through all 3 lps on hook.
Dc2tog [Yo, insert hook in st, yo and draw up a lp, yo, draw through 2 lps on hook] twice, yo and draw through all 3 lps on hook.

(colors A, B, C, D, E, F, and G)
Stripe Sequence Work 2 rows A, 1B, 2C, 3D, 1E, 2A, 3F, 1G

(ch a multiple of 12 sts + 3)
Note Work in *back* lps only throughout.
Row 1 Work 1 dc in 4th ch from hook, 1 dc in next 3 ch, [dc2tog over next 2 ch] twice, 1 dc in next 3 ch, 2 dc in next ch, *2 dc in next ch, 1 dc in next 3 ch, [dc2tog over next 2 ch] twice, 1 dc in next 3 ch, 2 dc in next ch; rep from * to end. Turn.
Row 2 Ch 1, 2 sc in first dc, 1 sc in next 3 dc, [sc2tog] twice, 1 sc in next 3 dc, 2 sc in next dc, *2 sc in next dc, 1 sc in next 3 dc, [sc2tog] twice, 1 sc in next 3 dc, 2 sc in next dc; rep from *, end last rep with 2 sc in top of t-ch. Turn.
Row 3 Ch 3 (counts as 1 dc), 1 dc in first sc, 1 dc in next 3 sc, [dc2tog] twice, 1 dc in next 3 sc, 2 dc in next sc, *2 dc in next sc, 1 dc in next 3 sc, [dc2tog] twice, 1 dc in next 3 sc, 2 dc in next sc; rep from * to end. Turn.
Rep rows 2 and 3, continuing stripe sequence.

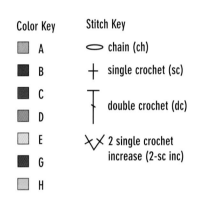

Color Key
- A
- B
- C
- D
- E
- G
- H

Stitch Key
- ⬭ chain (ch)
- + single crochet (sc)
- ⊤ double crochet (dc)
- ⋉⋊ 2 single crochet increase (2-sc inc)

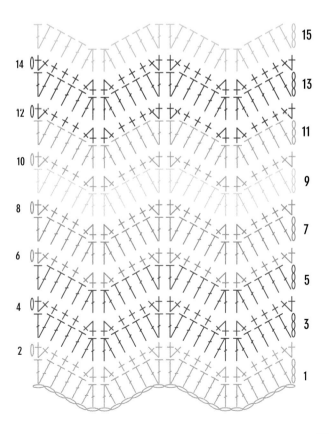

SLIPSTREAM

(colors A and B)

Stripe Sequence

Side 1 Work 1 row A, 2B, 2A

Side 2 Work 1 row A, 2B

Dc3(4)(7)tog [Yo, insert hook in st, yo and draw up a lp, yo, draw through 2 lps on hook] 3 (4) (7) times, yo and draw through all 4 (5) (8) lps on hook.

(ch a multiple of 10 sts + 7)

First Side

Row 1 With A, 1 sc in 2nd ch from hook, 1 sc in next ch, *skip 3 ch, 7 dc in next ch, skip 3 ch, 1 sc in next 3 ch; rep from *, end skip 3 ch, 4 dc in last ch. Turn.

Row 2 With B, ch 1, 1 sc in first 2 dc, *ch 3, dc7tog, ch 3, 1 sc in next 3 dc; rep from *, end ch 3, dc4tog. Turn.

Row 3 Ch 3 (counts as 1 dc throughout), 3 dc in first st, *skip next ch-3 sp, 1 sc in next 3 sc, skip ch-3 sp, 7 dc in next st; rep from *, end skip last ch-3 sp, 1 sc in last 2 sc. Turn.

Row 4 With A, ch 3, skip first sc, dc3tog, *ch 3, 1 sc in next 3 dc, ch 3, dc7tog; rep from *, end ch 3, 1 sc in last dc, 1 sc in top of t-ch. Turn.

Row 5 Ch 1, 1 sc in first 2 sc, *skip next ch-3 sp, 7 dc in next st, skip next ch-3 sp, 1 sc in next 3 sc; rep from *, end skip last ch-3 sp, 4 dc in last dc. Fasten off.

Second Side

Row 1 With WS and base ch facing, join A to first ch at right edge. Ch 1, 1 sc in first 2 ch, *skip next ch-3 sp, 7 dc in next ch, skip next ch-3 sp, 1 sc in next 3 ch; rep from *, end skip last ch-3 sp, 4 dc in last ch. Turn.

Rows 2 and 3 With B, rep rows 2 and 3 of First Side. Fasten off.

Color Key

- A
- B

Stitch Key

- chain (ch)
- single crochet (sc)
- double crochet (dc)

Second Side

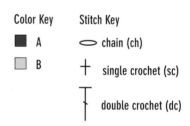

Opposite Side of Base Ch

First Side

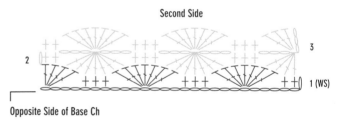

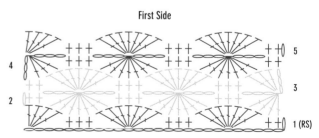

LACE RIPPLES

(colors A, B, C, and D)

Stripe Sequence 2 rows A, 2C, 2A, 2B

(ch a multiple of 16 sts + 2)

Row 1 With B, working in *back* lps only of foundation ch, 1 sc in 2nd ch from hook, *1 sc in next ch, ch 1, skip 1 ch, 1 hdc in next ch, ch 1, skip 1 ch, 1 dc in next ch, [ch 1, skip 1 ch, 1 tr in next ch] twice, ch 1, skip 1 ch, 1 dc in next ch, ch 1, skip 1 ch, 1 hdc in next ch, ch 1, skip 1 ch, 1 sc in next ch, ch 1, skip 1 ch; rep from *, end last rep 1 sc in last 2 ch. Turn.

Rows 2, 6, 10, and 14 With A, ch 1, 1 sc in each st and ch-1 sp. Turn.

Rows 3, 7, 11, and 15 With A, ch 1, 1 sc in each sc across. Turn.

Row 4 With C, ch 4 (counts as 1 tr), skip first st, *1 tr in next st, ch 1, skip 1 st, 1 dc in next st, ch 1, skip 1 st, 1 hdc in next st, [ch 1, skip 1 st, 1 sc in next st] twice, ch 1, skip 1 st, 1 hdc in next st, ch 1, skip 1 st, 1 dc in next st, ch 1, skip 1 st, 1 tr in next st, ch 1, skip 1 st; rep from *, end last rep 1 tr in last 2 sts. Turn.

Row 5 With C, ch 4 (counts as 1 tr), skip first st, *1 tr in next st, ch 1, skip 1 st, 1 dc in next st, ch 1, skip 1 st, 1 hdc in next st, [ch 1, skip 1 st, 1 sc in next st] twice, ch 1, skip 1 st, 1 hdc in next st, ch 1, skip 1 st, 1 dc in next st, ch 1, skip 1 st, 1 tr in next st, ch 1, skip 1 st; rep from *, end last rep 1 tr in last st, tr in top of t-ch. Turn.

Rows 8 and 9 With B, ch 1, 1 sc in first st, *1 sc in next st, ch 1, skip 1 st, 1 hdc in next st, ch 1, skip 1 st, 1 dc in next st, [ch 1, skip 1 st, 1 tr in next st] twice, ch 1, skip 1 st, 1 dc in next st, ch 1, skip 1 st, 1 hdc in next st, ch 1, skip 1 st, 1 sc in next st, ch 1, skip 1 st; rep from *, end last rep 1 sc in last 2 sts. Ch 1, turn.

Rows 12 and 13 With D, rep rows 4 and 5.

Rows 16 and 17 Rep row 8 and 9.

Rep rows 2–17.

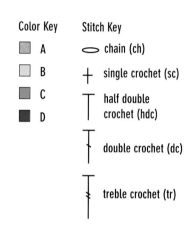

Color Key

- A
- B
- C
- D

Stitch Key

- ⬯ chain (ch)
- + single crochet (sc)
- T half double crochet (hdc)
- ⊤ double crochet (dc)
- ⊥ treble crochet (tr)

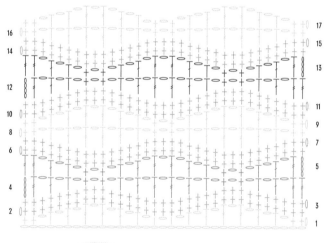

DIAGONAL STRIPES

(colors A and B)

(ch a multiple of 8 sts + 2)

Row 1 With A, 1 dc in 4th ch from hook and in next 2 ch, *with B, 1 dc in next 4 ch; with A, 1 dc in next 4 ch; rep from *, end with B, 1 dc in last 4 ch. Turn.

Row 2 With A, ch 3 (counts as 1 dc throughout), skip first st, *with B, 1 dc in next 4 sts; with A, 1 dc in next 4 sts; rep from *, end last rep with A, 1 dc in last 2 sts, 1 dc in top of t-ch. Turn.

Row 3 With A, ch 3, skip first st, 1 dc in next st, *with B, 1 dc in next 4 sts; with A, 1 dc in next 4 sts; rep from *, end last rep with A, 1 dc in last st, 1 dc in top of t-ch. Turn.

Row 4 With A, ch 3, skip first st, 1 dc in next 2 sts, *with B, 1 dc in next 4 sts; with A, 1 dc in next 4 sts; rep from *, end last rep with A, 1 dc in top of t-ch. Turn.

Row 5 With B, ch 3, skip first st, 1 dc in next 3 sts, *with A, 1 dc in next 4 sts; with B, 1 dc in next 4 sts; rep from *, end with A, 1 dc in last 3 sts, 1 dc in top of t-ch. Turn.

Row 6 With B, ch 3, skip first st, *with A, 1 dc in next 4 sts; with B, 1 dc in next 4 sts; rep from *, end last rep with B, 1 dc in last 2 sts, 1 dc in top of t-ch. Turn.

Row 7 With B, ch 3, skip first st, 1 dc in next st, *with A, 1 dc in next 4 sts; with B, 1 dc in next 4 sts; rep from *, end last rep with B, 1 dc in last st, 1 dc in top of t-ch. Turn.

Row 8 With B, ch 3, skip first st, 1 dc in next 2 sts, *with A, 1 dc in next 4 sts; with B, 1 dc in next 4 sts; rep from *, end last rep with B, 1 dc in top of t-ch. Turn.

Row 9 With A, ch 3, skip first st, 1 dc in next 3 sts, *with B, 1 dc in next 4 sts; with A, 1 dc in next 4 sts; rep from *, end with B, 1 dc in last 3 sts, 1 dc in top of t-ch. Turn.

Rep rows 2–9.

Color Key
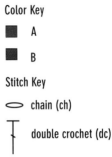
A

B

Stitch Key

chain (ch)

double crochet (dc)

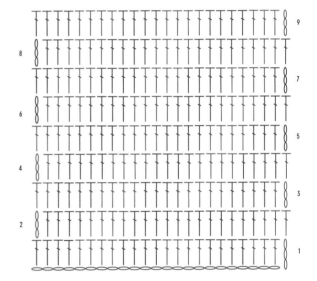

ST. GEORGE'S VARIATION

(colors A and B)

(ch a multiple of 14 sts + 9)

Row 1 With A, 1 dc in 4th ch from hook and in next 5 ch, *[with B, 1 dc in next ch; with A, 1 dc in next ch] 3 times; with B, 1 dc in next ch; with A, 1 dc in next 7 ch; rep from * to end. Turn.

Rows 2–4 With A, ch 3 (counts as 1 dc throughout), skip first st, 1 dc in next 6 dc, *[with B, 1 dc in next dc; with A, 1 dc in next dc] 3 times; with B, 1 dc in next st; with A, 1 dc in next 7 dc; rep from * across, end last rep with A, 1 dc in last 6 dc, 1 dc in top of t-ch. Turn.

Rows 5–8 With A, ch 3, skip first st, [with B, 1 dc in next dc; with A, 1 dc in next dc] 3 times; *with B, 1 dc in next 7 dc, [with A, 1 dc in next dc; with B, 1 dc in next dc] 3 times; with A, 1 dc in next dc; rep from * across, end last rep with A, 1 dc in top of t-ch. Turn.

Row 9 Rep row 2.

Rep rows 2–9.

Color Key

■ A

■ B

Stitch Key

⬭ chain (ch)

⊤ double crochet (dc)

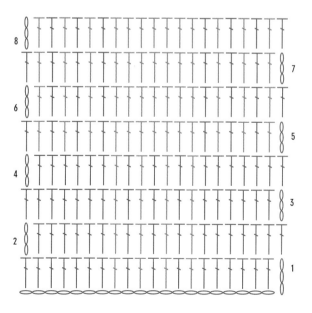

PLAY BLOCKS

(colors A, B, C, D, E, F, and G)

Stripe Sequence 2 rows A, 2B, 2C, 2A, 2D, 2E, 2F, 2G

FPtr (Front Post treble) Yo twice and insert hook from front to back to front around post of stitch two rows below (first row of previous color), yo and draw up a lp, [yo and draw through 2 lps on hook] 3 times.

(ch a multiple of 10 sts + 12)

Row 1 With A, 1 dc in 5th ch from hook and in each ch across. Turn.

Row 2 With A, ch 3 (counts as 1 dc throughout), skip first dc, 1 dc in each dc across, end 1 dc in top of t-ch. Turn.

Row 3 With B, ch 3, skip first dc, 1 dc in next dc, *[FPtr in next dc, 1 dc in next dc] 3 times, 1 dc in next 4 dc; rep from *, end last rep 1 dc in last dc, dc in top of t-ch. Turn.

Row 4 With B, rep row 2.

Row 5 With C, ch 3, skip first dc, 1 dc in next 6 dc, *[FPtr in next dc, 1 dc in next dc] 3 times, 1 dc in next 4 dc; rep from *, end 1 dc in last 2 dc, dc in top of t-ch. Turn.

Rep rows 2–5, continuing stripe sequence.

Stitch Key

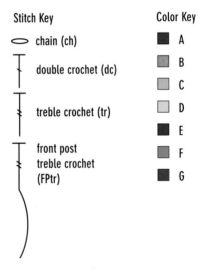

○ chain (ch)

† double crochet (dc)

‡ treble crochet (tr)

front post treble crochet (FPtr)

Color Key

A
B
C
D
E
F
G

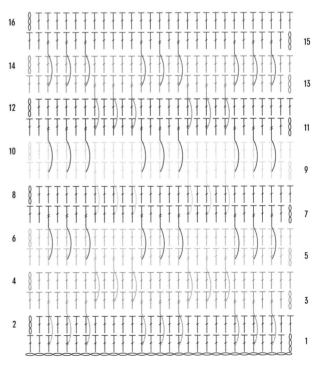

FILET

(ch a multiple of 2 sts + 6)

Row 1 Work 1 dc in 6th ch from hook, *ch 1, skip 1 ch, 1 dc in next ch; rep from * to end. Turn.

Row 2 Ch 4 (counts as 1 dc and ch 1), skip first dc and 1 ch, *1 dc in next dc, ch 1, skip 1 ch; rep from *, end 1 dc in 2nd ch of t-ch of row below. Turn.

Rep row 2.

MESH STITCH

(ch a multiple of 3 sts + 8)

Row 1 Work 1 dc in back lp of 8th ch from hook, *ch 2, skip 2 ch, 1 dc in back lp of next ch; rep from *, end 1 dc in back lp of last ch. Turn.

Row 2 Ch 5 (counts as 1 dc and ch 2), skip first dc and 2 ch, *1 dc in back lp of next dc, ch 2, skip 2 ch; rep from *, end 1 dc in 3rd ch of t-ch of row below. Turn.

Rep row 2.

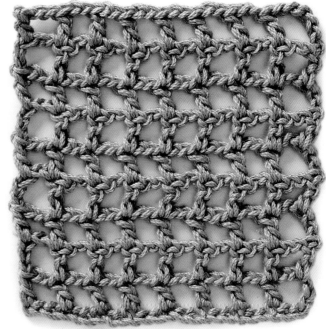

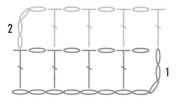

Stitch Key

- chain (ch)
- double crochet (dc)

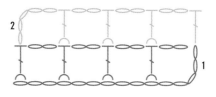

Stitch Key

- chain (ch)
- double crochet (dc)
- double crochet back loop only (dc back lp)

SHELL PATTERN

Shell (2 dc, ch 1, 2 dc)

(ch a multiple of 4 sts)
Row 1 Shell in 4th ch from hook, *skip 3 ch, shell in next ch; rep from * to end. Turn.
Row 2 Ch 3, *shell in ch-1 sp of next shell; rep from * to end. Turn.
Rep row 2.

VICTORY

V-st (Yo and draw up lp, yo and draw through 2 lps on hook) in first st, skip 1 st (or 3 ch), (yo and draw up lp, yo and draw through 2 lps) in next st (or ch), yo and draw through all 3 lps on hook.

(ch a multiple of 3 sts)
Row 1 Beg V-st in 4th ch from hook, *ch 3, V-st in last ch of previous V-st; rep from * to end. Turn.
Row 2 Ch 3, V-st in first V-st, *ch 3, V-st in last st of previous V-st; rep from *, end last rep with ch 3, V-st in last st of previous V-st and in top t-ch. Turn.
Rep row 2.

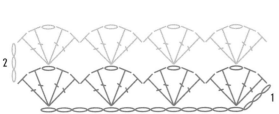

Stitch Key

⬭ chain (ch)

𝍖 double crochet (dc)

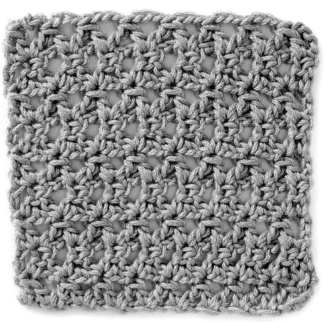

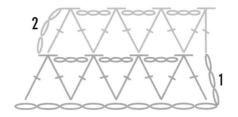

Stitch Key

⬭ chain (ch)

⋏ V-st

STACKED CLUSTERS

CL [Yo, insert hook in next dc, yo and draw up lp, yo and draw through 2 lps on hook] 5 times, yo and draw through all 6 lps on hook.

(ch a multiple of 6 sts + 3)

Row 1 (WS) 5 dc in 6th ch from hook, skip 2 ch, 1 dc in next ch, *skip 2 ch, 5 dc in next ch, skip 2 ch, 1 dc in next ch; rep from * to end. Turn.

Row 2 Ch 5, skip first dc, *CL over next 5 dc, ch 2, 1 dc in next dc, ch 2; rep from *, end CL over last 5 dc, ch 2, 1 dc in top of t-ch. Turn.

Row 3 Ch 3, skip 2 ch, 5 dc in CL, *skip 2 ch, 1 dc in next dc, skip 2 ch, 5 dc in next CL; rep from *, end skip 2 ch, 1 dc in 3rd ch of t-ch. Turn.

Rep rows 2 and 3.

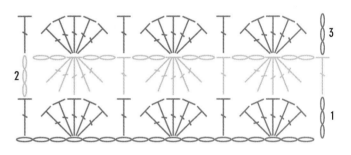

Stitch Key

⬯ chain (ch)

Ŧ double crochet (dc)

GILDED ARCHES

MP (make picot) (1 sc, ch 3, 1 sc)

(ch a multiple of 7 sts + 4)

Row 1 Work 1 hdc in 3rd ch from hook, 1 hdc in next 2 ch,
*ch 3, skip 2 ch, 1 sc in next ch, ch 3, skip 2 ch, 1 hdc in next
2 ch; rep from * to end. Turn.

Row 2 Ch 2, 1 hdc in first 2 hdc, *ch 3, MP in next sc, ch 3,
1 hdc in next 2 hdc; rep from * to end. Turn.

Row 3 Ch 1, 1 sc in first 2 hdc, *1 sc in next ch-3 sp, ch 5, skip
picot, 1 sc in same ch-3 sp as last sc, 1 sc in next 2 hdc; rep
from * to end. Turn.

Row 4 Ch 1, 1 sc in first 2 sc, *skip 1 sc, 7 sc in ch-5 sp, skip
1 sc, 1 sc in next 2 sc; rep from * to end. Turn.

Row 5 Ch 2, 1 hdc in first 2 sc, *ch 3, skip 3 sc, 1 sc in next sc,
ch 3, skip 3 sc, 1 hdc in next 2 sc; rep from * to end. Turn.
Rep rows 2–5.

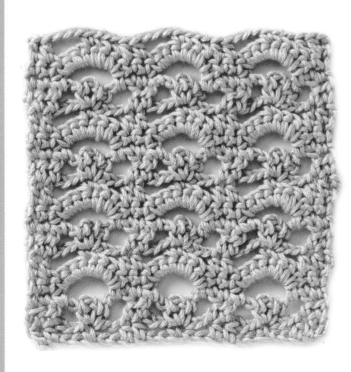

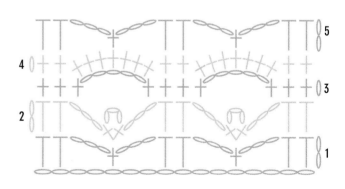

Stitch Key

⬭ chain (ch)

✛ single crochet (sc)

T half double
   crochet (hdc)

⋔ make picot (MP)
✕✕

CHEVRON MESH

Dc2tog [Skip next ch, yo, insert hook into next ch, yo, draw up a lp, yo and draw through 2 lps on hook] twice, yo and draw through all 3 lps on hook.

Dc3tog [Yo, insert hook in st, yo and draw up a lp, yo, draw through 2 lps on hook] 3 times, yo and draw through all 4 lps on hook.

(ch a multiple of 30 sts)

Row 1 Work 1 dc in 5th ch from hook, *[ch 1, skip 1 ch, 1 dc in next ch] 5 times, ch 1, skip 1 ch, ([1 dc, ch 1] twice, 1 dc) in next ch, [ch 1, skip 1 ch, 1 dc in next ch] 5 times, ch 1, dc2tog; rep from * to end. Turn.

Row 2 Ch 2 (counts as 1 dc), skip first dec, 1 dc in next dc, *[ch 1, 1 dc in next dc] 5 times, [ch 1, 1 dc] 3 times in next dc, [ch 1, 1 dc in next dc] 5 times, ch 1, CL; rep from * to end. Turn.
Rep row 2.

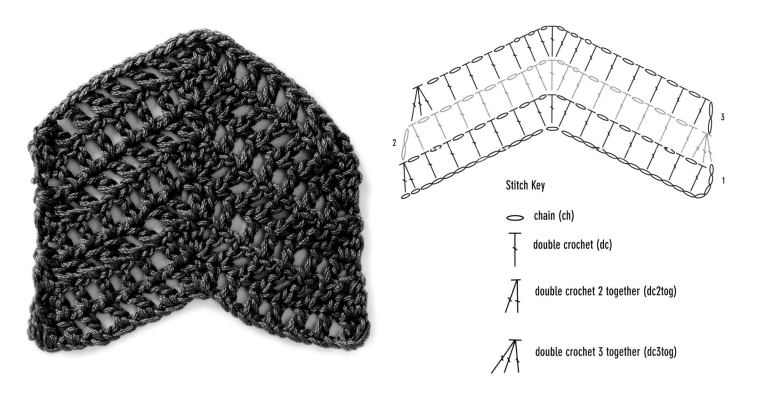

Stitch Key

⬭ chain (ch)

𝖳 double crochet (dc)

⋏ double crochet 2 together (dc2tog)

⋏ double crochet 3 together (dc3tog)

LONG LOOP MESH

Long dc Yo, insert hook in next ch, yo and draw up a ¾"/2cm long lp, [yo and draw through 2 lps on hook] twice.

(ch a multiple of 2 sts + 3)

Row 1 Long dc in 6th ch from hook, *ch 1, skip 1 ch, long dc in next ch; rep from * to end. Turn.

Row 2 Ch 4 (counts as 1 long dc and ch 1 throughout), skip first ch-1 sp, *long dc in next long dc, ch 1, skip next ch-1 sp; rep from *, end long dc in 3rd ch of ch-4 t-ch. Turn.
Rep row 2.

BERRY CLUSTERS

(ch a multiple of 3 sts + 4)

Row 1 Work 1 dc in 5th ch from hook, (ch 1, 1 dc) in same ch, *skip 2 ch, (1 dc, ch 1, 1 dc) in next ch; rep from *, end skip 1 ch, 1 dc in last ch. Turn.

Row 2 Ch 3, skip first dc, *(1 dc, ch 1, 1 dc) in next ch-1 sp; rep from *, end 1 dc in top of t-ch. Turn.
Rep row 2.

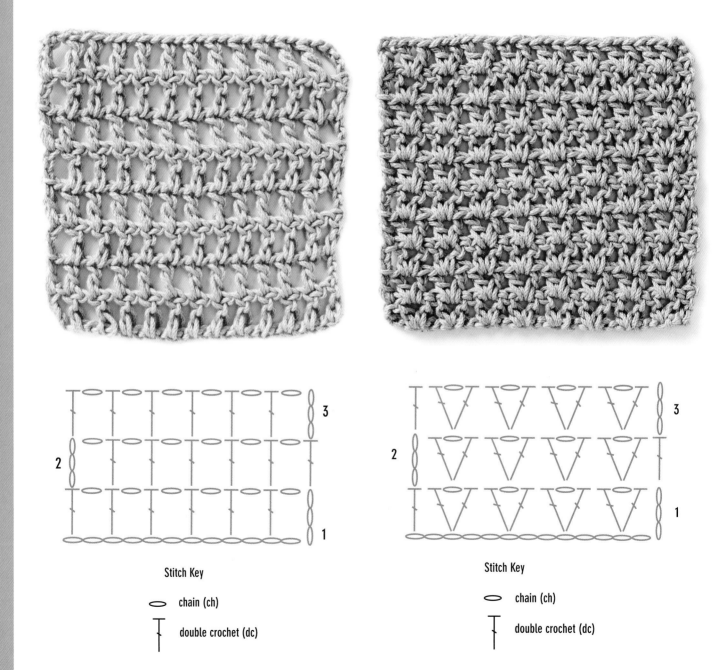

Stitch Key

⬭ chain (ch)

⊤ double crochet (dc)

CHECKERBOARD

(ch a multiple of 6 sts + 5)

Row 1 Work 1 sc in 2nd ch from hook and in each ch across. Turn.

Row 2 Ch 3 (counts as 1 dc throughout), skip first sc, 1 dc in next 3 sc, *ch 2, skip next 2 sc, 1 dc in next 4 sc; rep from * to end. Turn.

Row 3 Ch 5 (counts as 1 dc and ch 2), skip first dc, *skip next 2 dc, 1 dc in next dc, 2 dc in ch-2 sp, 1 dc in next dc, ch 2; rep from *, end skip last 2 dc, 1 dc in top of t-ch. Turn.

Row 4 Ch 3, *2 dc in ch-2 sp, 1 dc in next dc, ch 2, skip 2 dc, 1 dc in next dc; rep from *, end 2 dc in last ch-2 sp, 1 dc in 3rd ch of ch-5 t-ch. Turn.

Row 5 Rep row 3.

Row 6 Rep row 4.

Row 7 Ch 1, 1 sc in each dc and 2 sc in each ch-2 sp across, end 1 sc in top of t-ch. Turn.

Row 8 Ch 1, 1 sc in each sc across.

Rep rows 2–8.

Stitch Key

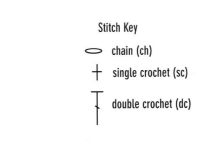

chain (ch)

single crochet (sc)

double crochet (dc)

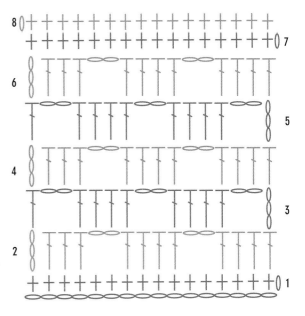

FANFARE

(ch a multiple of 6 sts + 4)

Row 1 Work 1 sc in 2nd ch from hook, 1 sc in next 2 ch, *ch 3, skip 3 ch, 1 sc in next 3 ch; rep from * across. Turn.

Row 2 Ch 1, 1 sc in first 2 sc, *skip 1 sc, 5 dc in ch-3 sp, skip 1 sc, 1 sc in next sc; rep from *, end 1 sc in last sc. Turn.

Row 3 Ch 4 (counts as 1 sc and ch 3), skip (2 sc, 1 dc), 1 sc in next 3 dc, *ch 3, skip (1 dc, 1 sc, 1 dc), 1 sc in next 3 dc; rep from * to last 4 sts, end ch 3, skip (1 dc, 1 sc), 1 sc in last sc. Turn.

Row 4 Ch 3 (counts as 1 dc), 3 dc in first ch-3 sp, *skip 1 sc, 1 sc in next sc, skip 1 sc, 5 dc in ch-3 sp; rep from *, end last rep 4 dc in last ch-3 sp. Turn.

Row 5 Ch 1, 1 sc in first 3 dc, *ch 3, skip (1 dc, 1 sc, 1 dc), 1 sc in next 3 dc; rep from * across. Turn.

Rep rows 2–5.

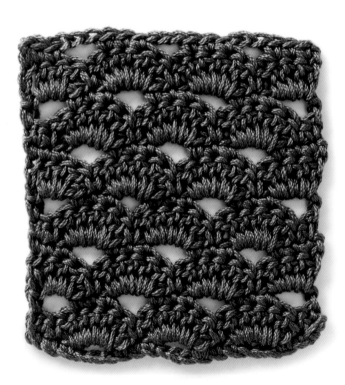

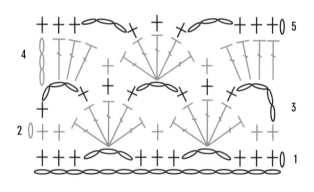

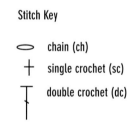

Stitch Key

⬯ chain (ch)

+ single crochet (sc)

⊤ double crochet (dc)

SPIKE WITH CHAIN LOOPS

(colors A and B)

Spike sc Insert hook approx 1"/2.5cm down from edge, yo, draw up a lp and complete as for sc.

(multiple of 12 sts + 2)

Row 1 (RS) With A, ch 1, *Spike sc in next st, ch 1, sl st in next st, ch 1; rep from * evenly across, end Spike sc in last st.
Row 2 (RS) With B, ch 1, 1 sc in first st, *ch 4, skip 2 sts, 1 sc in next st; rep from *, end 1 sc in last st.

DOUBLE HALF DOUBLE WITH PICOT

(colors A and B)

Picot (3-ch) Ch 3, sl st in 3rd ch from hook.

(multiple of 5 sts + 2)

Row 1 (RS) With A, ch 2, 1 hdc in first st, *skip 1 st, 2 hdc in next st; rep from * evenly across.
Row 2 (RS) With B, ch 1, 1 sc in first hdc, *Picot, 1 sc in next 4 hdc; rep from *, end Picot, 1 sc in last hdc.

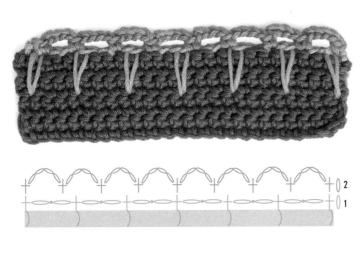

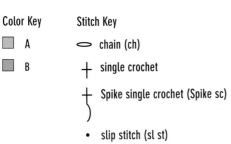

Color Key
- [ ] A
- [ ] B

Stitch Key
- ⬯ chain (ch)
- + single crochet
- ⸦ Spike single crochet (Spike sc)
- • slip stitch (sl st)

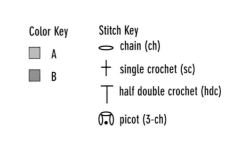

Color Key
- [ ] A
- [ ] B

Stitch Key
- ⬯ chain (ch)
- + single crochet (sc)
- T half double crochet (hdc)
- ⏝ picot (3-ch)

CHAIN AND ZIGZAG

(colors A and B)

Chain st Insert hook into work approx ½ "/1.3cm from edge, yo and draw lp to RS and through lp on hook.

Row 1 (RS) With A, working parallel to edge, make a slip knot, place on hook and hold yarn at WS, chain st evenly across.

Row 2 (RS) With B, make a slip knot, place on hook and hold yarn at WS, *(insert hook to WS then back to RS of work below chain, yo and draw up lp to RS, complete as for sc), ch 2, (insert hook to WS then back to RS of work in an angle above chain, yo and draw up lp to RS, complete as for sc), ch 2; rep from * evenly across, end 1 sc below chain st.

SINGLE CROCHET SLIP STITCH

(any multiple of sts + 1)

Row 1 (RS) Ch 1, 1 sc in each st across.

Right side of sample swatch

Row 2 (RS) Ch 1, sl st in each sc across.

Left side of sample swatch

Row 2 (RS) Ch 1, sl st in back lp of each sc across.

Color Key

▢ A

▨ B

Stitch Key

⌇ chain (ch)

+ single crochet (sc)

Stitch Key

⌇ chain (ch)

• slip stitch (sl st)

+ single crochet (sc)

DOUBLE CROCHET CHAIN

(multiple of 2 sts + 1)
Row 1 (RS) Ch 1, 1 sc in first and each st across.
Row 2 (RS) Ch 3, skip first sc, *1 dc in next sc, ch 1, skip 1 sc; rep from *, end 1 dc in last 2 sc.

TIPSY PICOT

Picot (3-ch) Ch 3, sl st in 3rd ch from hook.

(multiple of 3 sts + 2)
Row 1 (RS) Ch 1, 1 sc in first and each st across.
Row 2 (RS) Ch 1, 1 sc in first 3 sc, *Picot, 1 sc in 3 sc; rep from *, end last rep 1 sc in last 2 sc.

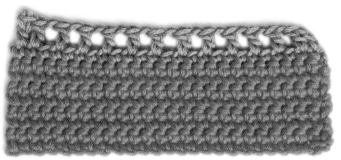

Stitch Key

⌒ chain (ch)

+ single crochet (sc)

⊤ double crochet (dc)

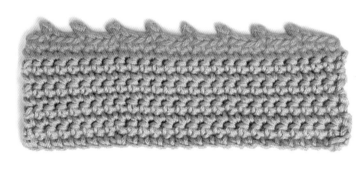

Stitch Key

⌒ chain (ch)

+ single crochet (sc)

🝐 picot (3-ch)

CHAIN PICOT EDGING

Picot (6-ch) Ch 6, sl st in 3rd ch from hook.

(any multiple of sts)
Row 1 (RS) Ch 1, 1 sc in edge, *Picot, ch 3, skip approx 1"/2.5cm along edge, 1 sc in edge; rep from * evenly across.

PEARL SHELL

CL (3-dc cluster) 3 dc in same st.

(multiple of 6 sts + 1)
Row 1 (RS) Ch 1, 1 sc in first and each st across.
Row 2 (RS) Ch 1, 1 sc in first 3 sc, *3 sc in next sc, 1 sc in 5 sc; rep from *, end last rep 1 sc in last 3 sc.
Row 3 (RS) Ch 3, skip 2 sc, *CL in center st of next 3-sc group, ch 2, skip 2 sc, 1 sc in next sc, ch 2, skip 2 sc; rep from *, end CL in center sc of last 3-sc group, ch 2, skip 2 sc, 1 sc in last sc.

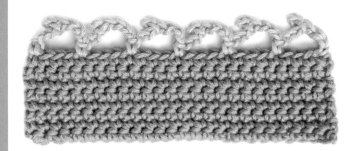

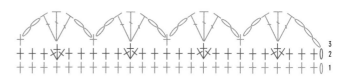

Stitch Key

⬭ chain (ch)

+ single crochet (sc)

(•) picot (3-ch)

Stitch Key

⬭ chain (ch)

+ single crochet (sc)

⩒ 3-double crochet cluster (cl)

DOUBLE CROCHET RUFFLE

(any multiple of sts)

Row 1 (RS) Ch 3 (counts as 1 dc throughout), 1 dc in same st as joining, 2 dc in each st across. Turn.

Row 2 Ch 3, skip first dc, 1 dc in each dc across, end dc in top of t-ch. Turn.

Row 3 Ch 3, 1 dc in first dc, 2 dc in each dc across, end 2 dc in top of t-ch. Turn.

Row 4 Rep row 2.

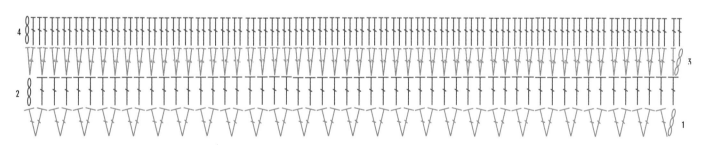

Stitch Key

⬭　chain (ch)

╀　single crochet (sc)

╿　double crochet (dc)

SCALLOP SHELL

(multiple of 4 sts + 1)

Row 1 (RS) Ch 1, 1 sc in first and each st across.

Row 2 (RS) Ch 1, 1 sc in first sc, *skip 1 sc, 5 dc in next sc, skip 1 sc, 1 sc in next sc; rep from * to end.

CROWN POINT

Bobble (3-tr) [Yo twice, insert hook into st, yo and draw up a lp, (yo and draw through 2 lps on hook) twice] 3 times, yo and draw through all 4 lps on hook.

Picot (3-ch) Ch 3, sl st in 3rd ch from hook.

(multiple of 7 sts)

Row 1 (RS) Ch 3, 1 dc in next and each st across.

Row 2 (RS) Ch 1, 1 sc in first dc, *ch 5, Bobble in next dc, Picot, skip 3 dc, Bobble in next dc, ch 5, 1 sc in next 2 dc; rep from *, end last rep, 1 sc in last dc.

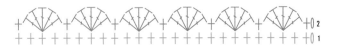

Stitch Key

⬯ chain (ch)

✛ single crochet (sc)

🇹 double crochet (dc)

Stitch Key

⬯ chain

✛ single crochet (sc)

🇹 double crochet (dc)

🇹 3-treble cluster (bobble)

picot (3-ch)

RUFFLED SHELL

CL3 (3-dc shell) 3 dc in same st.
CL5 (5-dc shell) 5 dc in same st.

(multiple of 6 sts + 1)
Row 1 (WS) Ch 1, 1 sc in first and each st across. Turn.
Row 2 (RS) Ch 3, CL3 in first sc, *1 sc in next sc, skip 1 sc, CL5 in next sc, skip 1 sc, 1 sc in next sc, CL5 in sc; rep from *, end last rep CL3 in last sc. Turn.
Row 3 Ch 1, 1 sc in first dc, skip 2 dc, *CL5 in next sc, skip 2 dc, 1 sc in 3rd dc of CL5; rep from *, end last rep 1 sc in 3rd dc of CL3.

STRING OF PEARLS

(colors A and B)
(multiple of 3 sts)
Rows 1 and 2 (RS) With A, ch 1, 1 sc in first and each st across.
Row 3 (RS) With B, *sl st in next 2 sc, (sl st, ch 3, 1 dc, ch 3, sl st) in next sc; rep from * to end.

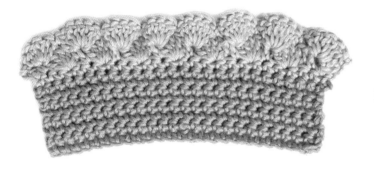

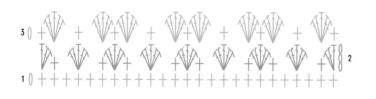

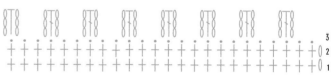

Stitch Key
⬭ chain (ch)
✚ single crochet (sc)
🕈 double crochet (dc)

Color Key
◼ A
◻ B

Stitch Key
⬭ chain (ch)
✚ single crochet (sc)
• slip stitch (sl st)
🕈 double crochet (dc)

COVERED BUTTON

Materials

Purchased button (button shown here is approx 1⅛"/28mm)

(ch 3 and join with sl st to form ring)

Rnd 1 Ch 2 (counts as 1 hdc throughout), 7 hdc in ring. Join with sl st to top of beg ch—8 hdc.

Rnd 2 Ch 2, working in back lps only, 1 hdc in same place as joining, work 2 hdc in each hdc around. Join with sl st to top of beg ch—16 hdc.

Rnds 3 and 4 Ch 2, working through back lps only, 1 hdc in each hdc around. Join with sl st to top of beg ch.

Rnd 5 Ch 1 (counts as 1 sc), working through back lps only, *skip next hdc, 1 sc in next 2 hdc; rep from * around—11 sc. Insert purchased button into crocheted cover. Join with sl st to top of beg ch.

Rnd 6 Ch 1, working through back lps only, *1 sc in next sc, skip 1 sc; rep from * around. Join with sl st to top of beg ch. Fasten off, leaving a 6"/15cm strand to sew on button. Thread strand in yarn needle. Use needle to weave around last rnd of sts. Pull to tighten, then fasten off securely.

Stitch Key

⊂⊃ chain (ch)

+ single crochet (sc)

T half double crochet (hdc)

T̯ half double crochet back loop only (hdc back lp)

• slip stitch (sl st)

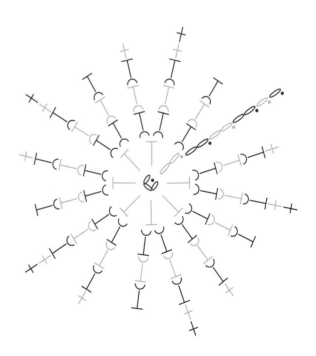

WILDFLOWER

(colors A, B, and C)

(with A, ch 4 and join with sl st to form ring)

Rnd 1 Ch 1, 11 sc in ring. Join with sl st to first sc.

Rnd 2 Ch 3 (counts as 1 dc), 1 dc in same place as joining, *ch 2, skip 1 sc, 2 dc in next sc; rep *, end ch 2. Join with sl st to top of beg ch-3. Fasten off.

Rnd 3 Join B with sl st in first ch-2 sp, ch 3 (counts as 1 dc), work (2 dc, ch 2, 3 dc) in same sp, *skip 1 dc, sl st in next dc, work (3 dc, ch 2, 3 dc) in next ch-2 sp; rep from *, end skip 1 dc. Join with sl st in next dc.

Rnd 4 3 sl sts up side edge of ch 3 of rnd 3, sl st across tops of first 2 dc, then sl st in ch-2 sp, ch 3 (counts as 1 dc), work 4 dc in same ch-sp, *1 tr in the next sl st, 5 dc in next ch-2 sp; rep from *, end 1 tr in last sl st of rnd 3. Join with sl st to top of beg ch-3 changing to C. Fasten off B.

Rnd 5 With C, ch 3, 1 dc in same place as joining, *[3 dc in next dc] twice, 2 dc in next dc, skip next dc, 1 sc in sp between last dc and next tr, 1 sc in sp between tr and next dc, 2 dc in next dc; rep from *, end last rep, omitting last 2 dc in next dc. Join with sl st in top of beg ch-3. Fasten off.

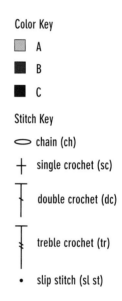

Color Key

▓ A

■ B

■ C

Stitch Key

⬭ chain (ch)

✛ single crochet (sc)

┼ double crochet (dc)

╪ treble crochet (tr)

• slip stitch (sl st)

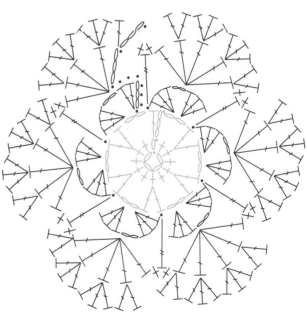

DAMASK ROSE

(ch 6 and join with sl st to form ring)

Rnd 1 *Ch 6, sl st in 5th ch from hook, ch 1, 1 sc in ring; rep from * 6 times more—7 petals. Do not join.

Rnd 2 Working behind petals of rnd 1, skip first sc, *ch 3, sl st around post of next sc; rep from * around—7 ch-3 lps. Do not join.

Rnd 3 [1 sc, 1 hdc, 6 dc, 1 sc] in each ch-3 lp around—7 petals. Do not join.

Rnd 4 Working behind petals of rnd 3, *ch 5, 1 sc in between next 2 sc (between petals); rep from * around—7 ch-5 lps. Do not join.

Rnd 5 [1 sc, (2 dc, ch 3, sl st in 3rd ch from hook—Picot) 3 times, 2 dc, 1 sc] in each ch-5 lp around.

Fasten off.

Stitch Key

◯ chain (ch)

✛ single crochet (sc)

┬ half double crochet (hdc)

┬ double crochet (dc)

• slip stitch (sl st)

⊙⊙ picot (3-ch)

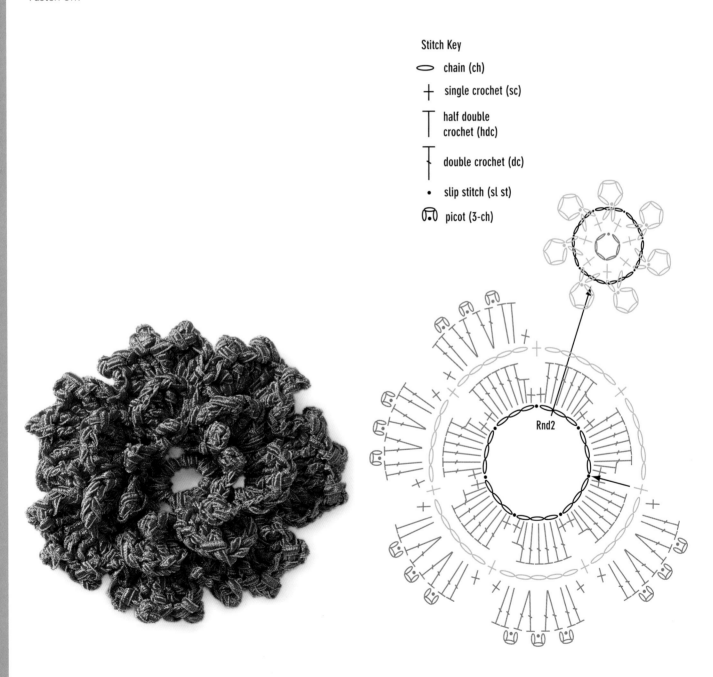

86

HYPERICUM

(colors A and B)

(with A, ch 8 and join with sl st to form ring)

Rnd 1 Ch 1, 12 sc in ring. Join with sl st to first sc.

Rnd 2 Ch 5 (counts as 1 sc and ch 4), *skip 1 sc, 1 sc in next sc, ch 4; rep from * around. Join with sl st in 2nd ch of beg ch-5 — 6 ch-4 lps.

Rnd 3 In each ch-4 lp, work (1 sc, 1 hdc, 3 dc, 1 hdc, 1 sc) — 6 petals. Join with sl st to first sc. Fasten off.

Rnd 4 With B and lp on hook, and working behind last rnd, *sc around post of sc on rnd 2, ch 5; rep from * around—6 ch-5 lps. Join with sl st to first sc. Fasten off.

Rnd 5 In each ch-5 lp, work (1 sc, 1 hdc, 5 dc, 1 hdc, 1 sc) — 6 petals. Join with sl st to first sc. Fasten off.

Color Key

■ A

▢ B

Stitch Key

⬭ chain (ch)

✛ single crochet (sc)

⊤ half double crochet (hdc)

⊤ double crochet (dc)

• slip stitch (sl st)

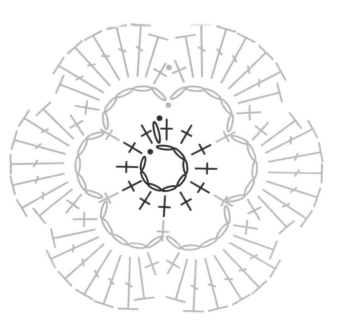

BUSY LIZZIE

(ch 5 and join with sl st to form ring)

Rnd 1 Ch 1 (counts as 1 sc), 15 sc in ring. Join with sl st to top of beg ch-2.

Rnd 2 [Ch 4, skip 2 sc, sl st in next sc] 5 times. Join with sl st in base of beg ch-4.

Rnd 3 In each ch-4 lp, work (1 sc, 3 dc, 1 tr, 3 dc, 1 sc)—5 petals. Join with sl st to first sc. Turn.

Rnd 4 [Ch 5, sl st between next 2 sc (between petals)] 5 times. Join with sl st to base of beg ch-5. Turn.

Rnd 5 Ch 1, work (1 sc, 4 dc, 2 tr, 4 dc, 1 sc) in each ch-5 sp around. Join with sl st to beg ch-1. Fasten off.

Stitch Key

⬭ chain (ch)

+ single crochet (sc)

⊤ double crochet (dc)

⧂ treble crochet (tr)

• slip stitch (sl st)

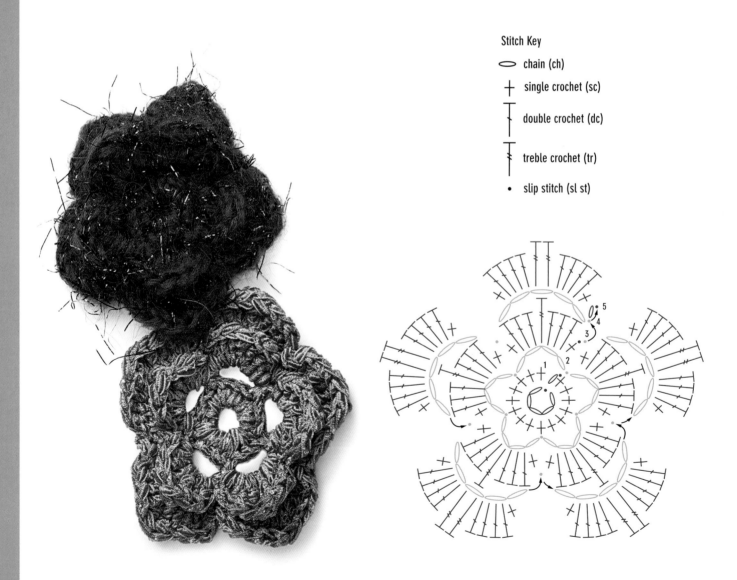

88

STARFISH

(colors A and B)

(with A, ch 5 and join with sl st to form ring)

Rnd 1 Ch 1, 10 sc in ring. Join with sl st to first sc.

Rnd 2 [Ch 8, 1 dc in 3rd ch from hook and in next 5 ch, skip next sc, sl st in next sc] 5 times. Fasten off.

Rnd 3 Join B in one skipped sc from rnd 2, *ch 3, sl st in next skipped sc from rnd 2; rep from * around. Join with sl st to base of beg ch-3 —5 ch-3 lps. Fasten off.

Color Key

■ A

▦ B

Stitch Key

⬯ chain (ch)

+ single crochet (sc)

T double crochet (dc)

• slip stitch (sl st)

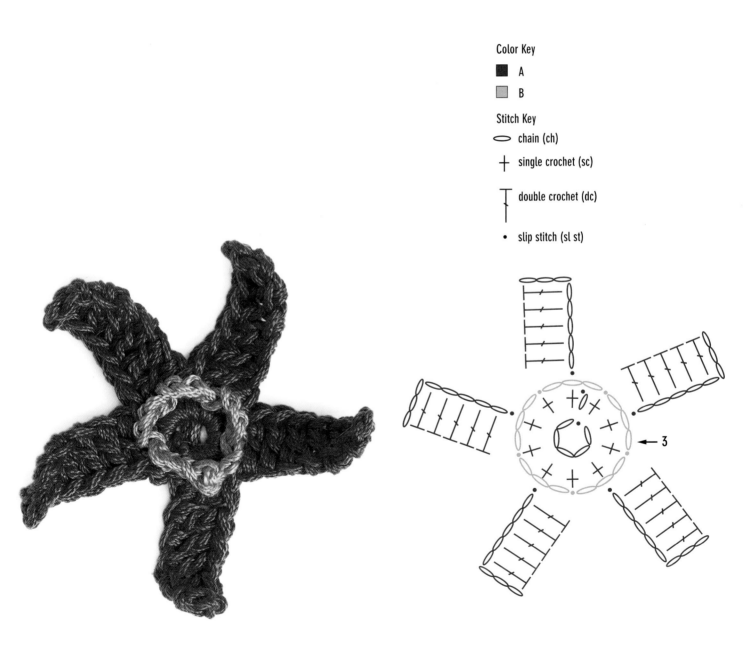

PROJECTS

You're now ready to take your newfound skills
and use them to stitch stunning crochet projects
—hats, cowls, bags, shawls, cardigans, and more—
all created by many of today's top crochet designers.

BOBBLE HAT

Perfect for a novice crocheter, Candi Jensen's quick-stitching slouch hat interjects a round of bobbles between rounds of double crochet.

●●
EASY

SIZE
Sized Small, Medium, and Large and shown in size Large.

FINISHED MEASUREMENTS
• Circumference 20½ (21¾, 23)"/50.5 (55.5, 58.5)cm
• Length 10"/25.5cm

MATERIALS
• 2 1.9oz/55g hanks (each approx 400yd/366m) of Jade Sapphire Exotic Fibers *2-ply Mongolian Cashmere* (cashmere) in #077 mallard 🔳
• One each size F/5 and G/6 (3.75 and 4mm) crochet hooks
OR SIZE TO OBTAIN GAUGE

GAUGE
14 sts and 9 rows = 4"/10cm over bobble pat using larger hook and 2 strands of yarn held tog.
TAKE TIME TO CHECK GAUGE.

NOTE
Work with 2 strands of yarn held tog throughout.

STITCH GLOSSARY
dc2tog (double crochet 2 tog) Yo and insert hook in next st, draw though a lp, yo and draw through 2 lps, (2 lps rem on hook), yo and insert hook in next st, draw through a lp, yo and draw through 2 lps, yo and pull through all 3 lps on hook.

BOBBLE PATTERN
Row 1 (RS) Hdc in each st. Ch 1, turn.
Row 2 Work hdc in first st, *ch 1, sk 1 st, hdc in each of next 3 sts; rep from *, end with hdc in last 2 sts, join with sl st. Ch 1, turn.
Row 3 Work hdc in each of next 2 hdc, *work bobble in next ch-1 sp, hdc in each of next 3 hdc; rep from *, end with hdc in last hdc, join with sl st. Ch 1, turn.
Row 4 Work dc in first hdc, *hdc in ch at top of bobble, dc in each of next 3 hdc; rep from *, end with dc in each of last 2 hdc, join with sl st. Ch 1, turn.

Rows 5 and 6 Work dc in each st around, join with sl st and ch 1, turn at end of each row.
Rep rows 1–6 for bobble pat.

Bobble
*Yo twice, insert hook in next st, pull up a lp, [yo, draw through 2 lps] twice (there are 2 lps on hook); rep from * 4 times more, yo and draw through all 6 lps on hook, ch 1.

HAT
For rib border, with smaller hook and 2 strands held tog, ch 4.
Row 1 Sc in 2nd ch from hook and in each ch across—3 sc. Ch 1, turn.
Row 2 Work sc in front lp only in each st. Ch 1, turn.
Rep row 2 for 70 (74, 78) rows more. Being careful not to twist piece, join final row with a sl st to foundation ch to form a circle, ch 1. Change to larger hook.
Row 1 Working along side of rib border, work hdc into each row end, join with sl st to first hdc—72 (76, 80) hdc. Ch 1, turn.
Note The main body of the hat is worked in rounds, joining each rnd with a sl st, and turning at the end of every rnd to keep the look of working back and forth in rows, but eliminating a seam. Beg with row 2, work in bobble pat through row 6, then rep rows 1–6 twice more. Piece measures approx 11½"/30cm from beg.

Shape crown
Note Work the crown in rnds without turning.
Dec rnd Work 2 dc tog around—36 (38, 40) sts.
Next rnd Rep dec rnd—18 (19, 20) sts.
Next rnd Work 2 dc tog around, end sc in last 0 (1, 0) st—9 (10, 10) sts.
Cut yarn, leaving a long tail. Draw tail through rem sts, pull tightly and secure.

FINISHING
Using 8"/20.5cm tail, sew ends of rib border tog. Push all bobbles out to RS. Work in ends.●

SHELL-STITCH COWL

A lacy shell-stitch pattern gives Yoko Hatta's casual cowl an enviable drape. It's an easy project, crocheted with subtly sequined yarn in a single long strip that is sewn together, then edged in chain stitch.

••
EASY

SIZE
Instructions are written for one size.

FINISHED MEASUREMENTS
Approx 8½ x 36"/21.5 x 91.5cm (before seaming)

MATERIALS
• 2 3½oz/100g balls (each approx 292yd/263m) of Universal Yarns *Bamboo Pop* (cotton/bamboo) in #106 turquoise ②
(*Original yarn:* Plymouth Yarn Company *Giada* in #35 blue.)
• Size G/6 (4mm) hook *OR SIZE TO OBTAIN GAUGE*

GAUGE
17½ sts and 11 rows = 4"/10cm over shell pat using size G/6 (4mm) hook.
TAKE TIME TO CHECK GAUGE.

STITCH GLOSSARY
9-st Shell (sh) Work ([dc, ch 1] 4 times, dc) into indicated st.
5-st Shell (sh) Work (2 dc, ch 1, 2 dc) into indicated st.

SHELL PATTERN
Row 1 Sc in 2nd ch from hook, [ch 3, sk 5 ch, work 9-st Shell in next ch, ch 3, sk 5 ch, sc in next ch] 3 times. Ch 3, turn.
Row 2 Work 2 dc in first sc, *ch 1, [sc in next ch-1 sp, ch 3] 3 times, sc in next ch-1 sp, ch 1, 5-st Shell in next sc; rep from * across, end last rep with ch 1, 3 dc in last sc. Ch 3, turn.
Row 3 2 dc in first dc, *ch 2, [sc in next ch-3 sp, ch 3] twice, sc in next ch-3 sp, ch 2, 5-st Shell in next ch-1 sp of shell; rep from * across, end last rep, ch 2, 3 dc in top of t-ch. Ch 3, turn.

Row 4 2 dc in first dc, *ch 3, [sc in next ch-3 sp, ch 3] twice, 5-st Shell in next ch-1 sp of shell; rep from * across, end last rep, ch 3, 3 dc in top of t-ch. Ch 1, turn.
Row 5 Sc in first dc, *ch 3, sk next ch 3, work 9-st Shell in next ch-3 sp, ch 3, sc in next ch-1 sp of shell; rep from * across, end ch 3, sc in top of t-ch. Ch 3, turn.
Rep rows 2–5 for shell pat.

COWL
Ch 38. Work row 1 in shell pat, then rep rows 2–5 for 24 times, then work rows 2 and 3 once more.
Joining row Hold work in a loop, being careful not to twist, so that the foundation ch is opposite the last row worked. Sl st in base of sc on foundation ch, 2 dc in first dc of working row, *ch 3, sk 1 ch-3 sp, sc in next ch-3 sp, ch 1, sl st in base of 9-st Shell on foundation ch, ch 1, sc in next ch-3 sp of working row, ch 3, 2 dc in next ch-1 sp, sl st in base of 5-st Shell on foundation ch, 2 dc in same ch-1 sp of working row; rep from * once, then ch 3, sk 1 ch-3 sp, sc in next ch-3 sp, ch 1, sl st in base of 9-st Shell on foundation ch, ch 1, sc in next ch-3 sp of working row, ch 3, 3 dc in top of t-ch, sl st in base of 3-dc shell on foundation ch. Do not fasten off.

Edging
Rnd 1 Sc in same sp as sl st just made, *ch 3, sc in base of next 3-dc shell. Rep from * around, ch 3, join rnd with sl st in 1st sc. Fasten off.
Rep edging on opposite side of cowl.•

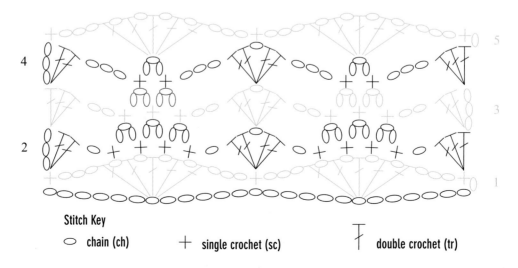

Stitch Key
○ chain (ch)   + single crochet (sc)   ⊤ double crochet (tr)

LACY JACKET

Casual details—slim-fitting long sleeves, an open front, and a scoop neckline—modernize the classic long-line silhouette of Deborah Newton's lacy jacket. The single-row double-crochet cluster-stitch fabric drapes to hug curves.

••
EASY

SIZE
Sized for Small, Medium, Large, X-Large, XX-Large and shown in size Medium.

FINISHED MEASUREMENTS
• Bust (closed) 34 (36, 38½, 40½, 43)"/86.5 (91.5, 98, 103, 109)cm
• Length 22½ (22½, 23, 23½, 24)"/57 (57, 58.5, 59.5, 61)cm
• Upper arm 11½ (11½, 12½, 13½, 14½)"/29 (29, 32, 34.5, 37)cm

MATERIALS
• 7 (8, 8, 9,10) 1¾oz/50g skeins (each approx 292yd/267m) Koigu Wool Designs Lace Merino (wool/nylon) in #601 orange/purple multi (0)
• One size F/5 (3.75mm) crochet hook OR SIZE TO OBTAIN GAUGE

GAUGE
30 sts and 14 rows = 4"/10cm over lacy box pat st using size F/5 (3.75mm) crochet hook.
TAKE TIME TO CHECK GAUGE.

LACY BOX PATTERN STITCH
Chain a multiple of 4 plus 4.
Row 1 Work 3 dc in 4th ch from hook, *sk 3 ch, work (1 sc, ch 3, 3 dc) in next ch; rep from *, end sk 3 ch, 1 sc in last ch, turn.
Row 2 Ch 3, work 3 dc in first st, *(1 sc, ch 3, 3 dc) in ch-3 lp; rep from *, end 1 sc in last t-ch lp, turn.
Rep row 2 for lacy box pat st.
When sts are described, the ch 3 and 3 dc in each box pat counts as 4 sts.
To dec in pat st To dec 1 (2) sts at beg of row, work 1 (2) less dc in the first box group of 3 dc; to dec 1 (2) sts at end of row, work 1 (2) less dc in the last box group of (sc, ch 3, 3 dc). Maintain the pat st when possible, otherwise work in dc only.
To inc in pat st Inc in dc only at beg or end of row until there are 4 plain dc, then work added sts into box pat.

BACK
Ch 132 (140, 148, 156, 164).
Work row 1 of lacy box pat st—32 (34, 36, 38, 40) box pat sts.
Cont in box pat st until piece measures 15"/38cm from beg.

Armhole shaping
Row 1 (RS) Work to the last 2 pats (or 8 sts), sc in the ch-lp, turn leaving the 2 pats unworked.
Row 2 Rep row 1—28 (30, 32, 34, 36) box pats.

Dec row 3 (RS) Work 1 less dc at beg and end of row.
Next row Work even.
Rep the last 2 rows 7 times more—24 (26, 28, 30, 32) box pats. Work even until armhole measures 5½ (5½, 6, 6½, 7)"/14 (14, 15, 16.5, 18)cm.

Neck shaping, right shoulder
Mark the center 10 box pats.
Next row (RS) Work in pat st to the center marked sts, turn leaving rem sts unworked.
Next row (WS) Work in pat st to end.
Dec row (RS) Work to last box pat, turn leaving this pat unworked. Work 1 row even.
Rep the last 2 rows once more—5 (6, 7, 8, 9) pats rem for shoulder. Work even until armhole measures 7½ (7½, 8, 8½, 9)"/19 (19, 20.5, 21.5, 23)cm. Fasten off.

Left shoulder
Join yarn at the left of the marked neck sts and work as for right shoulder, reversing shaping.

LEFT FRONT
Ch 68 (72, 76, 80, 84).
Work row 1 of lacy box pat st—16 (17, 18, 19, 20) box pat sts. Cont in box pat st until piece measures 15"/38cm from beg, end with a RS row.

Armhole shaping
Next row (WS) Work to the last 2 pats (or 8 sts), turn leaving these 2 pats unworked—14 (15, 16, 17, 18) box pat sts.
Dec row (RS) Work 1 less dc at beg of row.
Rep dec row every other row 7 times more—12 (13, 14, 15, 16) box pat sts, AT SAME TIME, when armhole measures 4 (4, 4½, 5, 5½)"/10 (10, 11.5, 12.5, 14)cm, work as foll:

Neck shaping
Next row (RS) Work to last 6 box pats, turn leaving these sts unworked.
Work 1 row even.
Dec 1 dc at end of every RS row until 1 more box pat has been eliminated—5 (6, 7, 8, 9) box pats rem. Work even until armhole measures same as back to shoulder. Fasten off.

RIGHT FRONT
Work as for left front, reversing all shaping.

SLEEVES

Ch 64 (64, 72, 80, 88).

Work row 1 of lacy box pat st—15 (15, 17, 19, 21) box pat sts.

Work in box pat st for 3 rows more.

Inc row (RS) Inc 1 dc at beg and end of row.

Note Work the inc'd sts in dc only until 4 dc have been added each side, then work inc'd sts in box pat.

Rep inc row every 4th row 11 times more—21 (21, 23, 25, 27) box pat sts. Work even until piece measures 17½"/44.5cm from beg.

Cap shaping

Rows 1 and 2 Work same as for back armhole shaping—17 (17, 19, 21, 23) box pat sts. Then keeping to pat as before, dec 2 dc at beg only of the next 16 rows, then dec 2 dc at beg and end of the next 0 (0, 2, 4, 6) rows—9 box pat sts.

Fasten off.

FINISHING

Sew shoulder seams. Set in sleeves. Sew side and sleeve seams.

Outer trim

Join yarn in one side seam, work 1 sl st, *sk approx ¼"/.5cm, work 5 tr in next st or space, sk approx ¼"/.5cm, work sl st in next st or space; rep from * around entire outer edge of jacket, working 8 tr in each corner. Join and fasten off. Work sleeve trim in same way.•

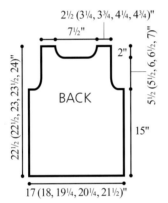

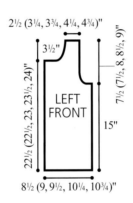

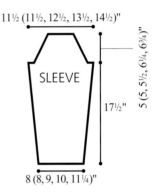

DRAWSTRING BAG

With its flapper-esque embellishment of tasseled fringe, Mary Jane Hall's lacy drawstring bag lends attitude to any outfit. Adaptable in size, it's crocheted in cotton/linen and lined with fabric that peeks through the openwork.

••
EASY

FINISHED MEASUREMENTS
Approx 13½"/34cm wide x 16"/40.5cm tall (without handles)

MATERIALS
• 3 1¾oz/50g hanks (each approx 160yd/146m) of The Fibre Company/Kelbourne Woolens *Savannah* (wool/cotton/linen/soya) in natural ❷
• Size F/5 (3.75mm) crochet hook *OR SIZE TO OBTAIN GAUGE*
• ⅓yd/.3m fabric for inside lining; ⅓yd/.3m contrasting fabric for outside lining (or ⅔yd/.6m of one color)
• Thread to match fabric and sewing needle
• 2 wooden beads with holes large enough for needle to go through
• 2 leather handles, 10"/25.5cm long when folded
• Yarn needle, rustproof pins, spray bottle

GAUGE
One 14-st rep = 3"/7.5cm and 8 rnds = 4"/10cm over V-st pat using size F/5 (3.75mm) hook.
TAKE TIME TO CHECK GAUGE.

NOTES
Bag begins at top edge and is worked in the round. For a wider bag, add to base ch in multiples of 14.

STITCH GLOSSARY
V-st Work tr, ch 3, tr in one st.
Bean stitch picot Ch 2, yo, [insert hook in 2nd ch from hook and pull up a ¼"/.5cm lp] 3 times, yo and draw through all lps on hook. This will look like a small puff st lying sideways.

BAG
Ch 126, being careful not to twist ch, sl st to first ch forming a ring.

Beg V-st pat
Rnd 1 Ch 1, sc in each ch around, sl st to first sc—126 sc.
Rnd 2 Ch 1, sc in first 5 sc (includes sp with sl st), *ch 3, sk 4 sc, V-st in next sc, ch 3, sk 4 sc, sc in next 5 sc; rep from * around, sl st to first sc—9 V-sts.
Rnd 3 Sl st over to middle sc, ch 1, sc in same sp, *3 tr in ch-3 sp, tr in next tr, 3 tr in ch-3 sp, tr in next tr, 3 tr in ch-3 sp, sk 2 sc, sc in next sc; rep from *, sl st to first sc.
Rnd 4 Ch 7 (counts as tr + ch 3), tr in same sp, *ch 3, sk 3 tr, tr in next 5 tr, ch 3, V-st in next sc; rep from *, end with ch 3, sl st in ch-4 of ch-7—9 V-sts.
Rnd 5 Ch 4 (counts as tr), *3 tr in ch-3 sp, tr in next tr, 3 tr in

ch-3 sp, sk 2 sc, sc in next sc, sk 2 sc, 3 tr in ch-3 sp, tr in next tr; rep from *, end with 3 tr in ch-3 sp, sl st to top of ch-4.
Rnd 6 Ch 1, sc in same sp and in next 4 tr, *ch 3, V-st in next sc, ch 3, sk 3 tr, sc in next 5 tr; rep from *, end with ch 3, sl st to first sc. Rep rnds 3–6 for V-st pat until 32 rows have been worked from beg, end with a pat rnd 5. Fasten off. This will be lower edge of bag. Steam block bag.

BASE
Rnd 1 With last rnd facing, attach yarn in 2nd tr to right of any sc on rnd. Ch 1, including sp with sl st, *hdc in next 2 tr, 2 dc in sc, hdc in next 2 tr, sc in next 7 tr; rep from * around, sl st to hdc.
Rnd 2 Ch 1, sc in each st around, adding extra sts if needed to

keep work flat. Sl st to first st, turn bag inside out. Place bag on a flat surface with RS tog, line up sts and pin opening. Work sc across for seam. Fasten off, turn bag RS out.

Top edge

Rnd 1 With top edge of RS facing, attach yarn to st at right of any V-st, ch 4 (counts as dc + ch 1), sk 1 sc, dc in next 5 sc, *ch 1, sk next sc, dc in next 6 dc; rep from * around, sl st to ch-3 of ch-4.
Rnd 2 Ch 3, dc in each st around, sl st to top of ch-3—126 sts.
Rnd 3 Ch 3, dc in next 5 dc, *dc in next 6 dc, work Bean st picot, dc in same st as last dc; rep from * around, end with dc in last 7 dc, work Bean st picot, sl st to top of ch-3—21 Bean st picots. Fasten off.

Drawstring

Ch 150, sl st in 2nd ch from hook and in each ch to end—149 sl sts. Fasten off, leaving a 4"/10cm tail. Weave drawstring through ch-1 sps of rnd 1. Place wood bead on each end with yarn and needle. Tie a double knot to hold bead in place.

LINING

Note Bag has a double lining so RS of fabric shows through the front as well as the inside.

Body

Measure each side of the bag and add a seam allowance of about ½"/1.5cm and cut pieces to this measurement as foll:

Inside lining

2 pieces: 15"/38cm long x 11½"/29cm wide (front and back);
2 pieces: 15"/38cm long x 4½"/11.5cm wide (sides);
1 piece: 4½"/11.5cm deep x 11½"/29cm wide (bottom)

Pocket

Pocket has double fabric to avoid frayed edges.
Cut 2 squares of fabric 5½"/14cm x 6½"/16.5cm. Press all 4 edges under ½"/1.5cm to WS on both pocket pieces. With WS tog, pin both pocket pieces to each other, and then pin pocket where desired to one side of lining that will be showing on inside of bag. Stitch in place, close to edges, leaving top edge free for pocket opening.
With RS tog, sew all 4 side seams, one at a time, leaving ½"/1.5cm open at lower edges. This will prevent puckering and make it easier to pin and sew bottom to body of lining.

Lower edge

Matching up seams, pin and sew lower edges to lower edges of body, one at a time, leaving ½"/1.5cm opening on all corners.

Outside lining

For a double lining with contrasting fabric showing through lace on outside, repeat steps above. Pin both linings with WS together at top edges, and sew approx ⅛–¼"/.2–.5cm from folded edge. Place lining inside bag, making sure sides of lining are at sides of bag. Hand or machine sew lining to bag at top edge.

FINISHING

Weave in loose ends and attach handles to top of bag with yarn or thread as in photo.

Tassel fringe

Cut 258 pieces of yarn each 7"/17.5cm long. For 1 tassel, fold 6 pieces tog, pull through desired st on bag with hook, same as you would fringe. Rep for all tassels and trim to approx 2–2¼"/5–5.5cm.•

MOCK HAIRPIN WRAP

Narrow double-crochet strips, worked with chain loops along either edge, form the foundation of Jill Wright's airy mock-hairpin wrap.

●●●
INTERMEDIATE

SIZE
Instructions are written for one size.

FINISHED MEASUREMENTS
Approx 20 x 68"/51 x 172.5cm

MATERIALS
• 3 balls (each approx 300yd/274m) of Aunt Lydia's *Crochet Thread Bamboo 10* (viscose from bamboo) in #226 natural (A) **(0)**
• 1 ball in #320 mushroom (B)
• Size 1.8mm steel crochet hook *OR SIZE TO OBTAIN GAUGE*

GAUGE
• 28 dc and 12 rows = 4"/10cm over dc using size 1.8mm hook. *TAKE TIME TO CHECK GAUGE.*

NOTE
Wrap is worked as 5 strips that are joined as they are worked. Each strip begins with a spine that is worked back and forth, then 2 rnds of lace are worked around the spine.

STRIP 1
Spine
With A, ch 22.
Row 1 (WS) Sk 14 ch, dc in next ch, ch 1, sk 1 ch, dc in next 4 ch, ch 1, sk 1 ch, dc in last ch.
Row 2 Ch 14, dc in first dc, ch 1, sk ch-1 sp, dc in next 4 dc, ch 1, sk ch-1 sp, dc in last dc.
Rep row 2 for 200 times—101 ch-14 sps on each side of spine.

Lace
With RS facing, join B with a sl st to first dc of final row of spine.
Lace rnd 1 (RS) Ch 1, sc in same dc as join, sc in ch-1 sp, sc in next 4 dc, sc in ch-1 sp, sc in next dc, ch 8, working along long

edge of spine, insert hook in first 3 ch-14 sps and sc tog, *[ch 8, twist next ch-14 sp and 3 sc in top] 5 times, ch 8, insert hook in next 5 ch-14 sps and sc tog; rep from * to last 8 ch-14 sps, [ch 8, twist next ch-14 sp and 3 sc in top] 5 times, ch 8, insert hook in next 3 ch-14 sps and sc tog, ch 8, sc in unused lp of 8 foundation chs along edge of spine, working along opposite edge of spine, [ch 8, twist next ch-14 sp and 3 sc in top] 3 times, **ch 8, insert hook in next 5 ch-14 sps and sc tog, [ch 8, twist next ch-14 sp and 3 sc in top] 5 times; rep from ** to last 8 ch-14 sps, ch 8, insert hook in next 5 ch-14 sps and sc tog, [ch 8, twist next ch-14 sp and 3 sc in top] 3 times, ch 8, join with a sl st in first sc.
Lace rnd 2 Ch 1, sc in first sc, ch 8, sk 6 sc, sc in next sc, *ch 8, sc in next ch-8 sp; rep from * to foundation edge of spine, ch 8, sc in first sc of foundation edge, sk 6 sc, sc in next sc, rep between *'s along opposite edge to beg of rnd, ch 8, join with a sl st in first sc. Fasten off.

STRIP 2
Work spine and Lace rnd 1 as for Strip 1.
Lace rnd 2 (joining rnd) Ch 1, sc in first sc, ch 8, sk 6 sc, sc in next sc, ch 8, sc in next ch-8 sp, *ch 4, sc in corresponding ch-8 sp in Lace rnd 2 of previous strip, ch 4, sc in next ch-8 sp on current strip; rep from * to last 2 ch-8 sps before foundation edge of spine, ch 8, sc in next ch-8 sp, ch 8, sc in first sc along foundation edge, ch 8, sk 6 sc, sc in next sc, **ch 8, sc in next ch-8 sp; rep from ** to beg of rnd, ch 8, join with sl st in first sc. Fasten off.

STRIPS 3–5
Work as for strip 2. Do not fasten off last strip.

EDGING
Rnd 1 (RS) Ch 1, work 10 sc in each ch-8 sp and 5 sc in center join sps around, join with sl st in first sc. Fasten off.●

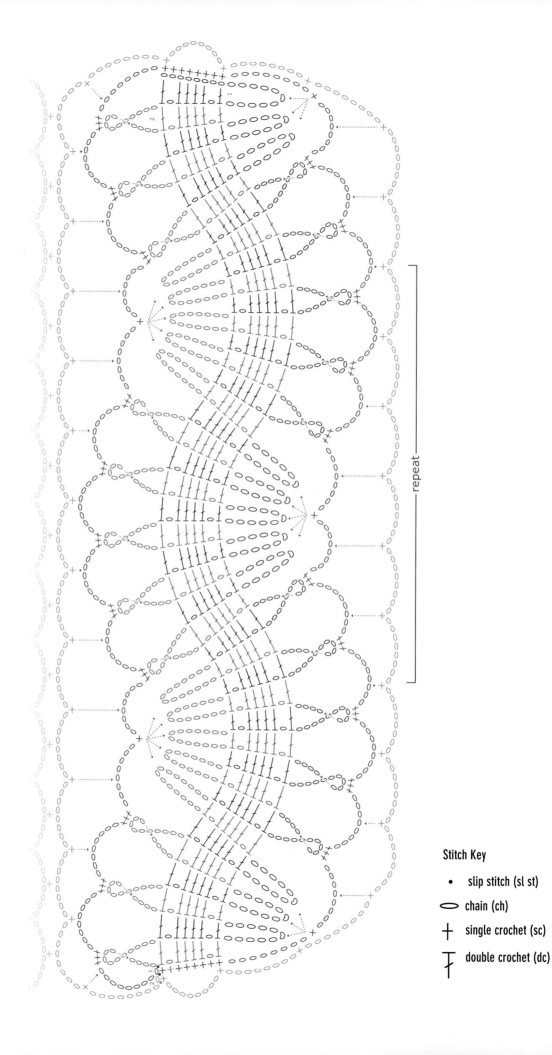

STRIP 1 DIAGRAM

Stitch Key

- slip stitch (sl st)
- chain (ch)
- single crochet (sc)
- double crochet (dc)

SHELL-STITCH JACKET

Kathy Merrick's jacket is worked in one-row stripes of shell stitch, exquisitely offsetting the icy gleam of the mohair and silk yarn. It's crocheted in one piece from the stand-up collar down to the armholes, using increases to shape the raglan-style yoke, before being divided for the body and sleeves.

●●●
INTERMEDIATE

SIZE
Sized for Small, Medium, Large and shown in size Medium.

FINISHED MEASUREMENTS
- Bust 42 (48, 54)"/106.5 (122, 137)cm
- Waist 34 (40, 44)"/86 (101.5, 111.5)cm
- Upper arm 14 (16, 17½)"/35.5 (40.5, 44.5)cm
- Length 31½ (34½, 35½)"/80 (87.5, 90)cm

MATERIALS
- 2 .88oz/25g skeins (each approx 230yd/210m) of Rowan *Kidsilk Haze* (mohair/silk) each in #649 brick (B), #666 alhambra (C), #667 tornado (E), #589 majestic (H), and #582 trance (I)
- 1 (2, 2) skeins each in #605 smoke (A), #600 dewberry (D), #652 mud (F), and #583 blushes (G)
- Size D/3 (3.25mm) hook *OR SIZE TO OBTAIN GAUGE*
- Stitch markers
- 5 (6, 6) 1½"/38mm buttons
- One ½"/12mm button
- ½yd/.5m gray felt
- Tapestry needle

GAUGE
6 shell sts and 10 rows = 4"/10cm over shell pat using size D/3 (3.25mm) hook.
TAKE TIME TO CHECK GAUGE.

NOTES
1 Jacket is worked from the neck down in rows to armholes, then is divided into body and sleeves to finish.
2 To inc, work 2 shell sts in indicated ch-3 sp.
3 Change to new color by working the last 2 lps of the last row before color change with new color.

SHELL PATTERN
Chain a multiple of 6 plus 1.
Setup row 2 dc into 4th ch from hook (counts as ch 3, 2 dc), *sk 2 ch, sc into next ch, sk 2 ch, ch 3, 3 dc into next ch; rep from * to last ch, sc in last ch, turn.
Row 1 Ch 3, 2 dc into first sc, work shell st (sc, ch 3, 3 dc) in each ch-3 sp across, sc into top of t-ch, turn.
Rep row 1 for shell pat.

STRIPE SEQUENCE
*Work 1 row each A, B, C, D, E, F, G, H, I; rep from * (9 rows) for stripe sequence.

BODY
With A, ch 97.
Work setup row of st pat, change to B. Place stitch markers in sc between pat reps 2 and 3, 5 and 6, 11 and 12, 14 and 15—16 pat reps.
Inc row (RS) Inc in first ch-3 sp, *work in shell pat to 1 shell before next marker, inc in next ch-3 sp, move marker up, inc in next ch-3 sp; rep from * 3 times more, work shell pat to last ch-3 sp, inc in last ch-3 sp, work to end, changing to C—26 pat reps.
Next row (WS) Inc in first ch-3 sp, work shell pat to last ch-3 sp, inc in last ch-3 sp, changing to D—28 pat reps.
Cont stripe sequence throughout, rep last 2 rows 3 (4, 4) times—64 (76, 76) pat reps.
Next row (RS) *Work shell pat to one rep before next marker, inc in next ch-3 sp, move marker up, inc in next ch-3 sp; rep from * 3 times more, work to end—72 (84, 84) pat reps.

Next row (WS) Work even in shell pat.
Rep last 2 rows 4 (4, 5) times—104 (116, 124) pat reps.

Separate body and sleeves
Row 1 (RS) Work shell pat to first marker, ch 6 (6, 12), sk sleeve sts to 2nd marker, work across back in shell pat to 3rd marker, ch 6 (6, 12), sk sleeve sts to 4th marker, work from 4th marker to end.
Row 2 (WS) *Work shell pat to ch-6 (ch-6, ch-12), **sk 2 ch, sc into next ch, ch 3, 3 dc into next ch; rep from ** 0 (0, 2) times; rep from * once more, work shell pat to end—64 (72, 80) pat reps.
Work even until piece measures 4"/10cm from underarm, ending with WS row. Place markers between pat reps 20 and 21 (23 and 24, 24 and 25), and between pat reps 43 and 44 (49 and 50, 56 and 57).

Waist shaping
Dec row (RS) Work even in pat to 2 pat reps before first marker, *(sc, ch 3) in next ch-3 sp, 3 dc in next ch-3 sp**, rep from * to ** once, moving marker up, work even in pat to 2 pat reps before second marker, rep from * to ** twice, moving marker up, work even in pat to end—60 (68, 76) pat reps.
Work even in pat for 7 (7, 9) rows more. Rep dec row—56 (64, 72) pat reps.
Work even in pat for 5 (7, 7) rows more.
Inc row (RS) Work even in pat to 1 pat rep before first marker, inc in next 2 pat reps, moving marker up, work even in pat to 1 pat rep before 2nd marker, inc in next 2 pat reps, moving marker up, work even in pat to end—60 (68, 76) pat reps.
Work even in pat for 7 (9, 9) rows more. Rep inc row—64 (72, 80) pat reps.
Work even in pat until piece measures 20 (22, 22)"/51 (56, 56)cm from underarm. Fasten off.

SLEEVES
Beg at underarm ch-6 (ch-6, ch-12) and working into opposite side of chain, join yarn continuing stripe sequence to work across chain.
Row 1 (RS) Ch 1, [sc in next ch, ch 3, 3 dc in next ch, sk 2 ch] 1 (1, 3) times, work even in pat to end, turn—22 (24, 28) pat reps.

Work even in pat 3 more rows.
Dec row (RS) Work even in pat to 2nd pat rep, (sc, ch 3) in next ch-3 sp, 3 dc in next ch-3 sp, work even in pat to last 3 pat reps, (sc, ch 3) in next ch-3 sp, 3 dc in next ch-3 sp, work even to end—20 (22, 26) pat reps.
Work even in pat for 5 (7, 7) rows more. Rep dec row—18 (20, 24) pat reps.
Rep last 6 (8, 8) rows 3 (3, 4) times more—12 (14, 16) pat reps.
Work even until sleeve measures 16 (17, 18)"/40.5 (43, 45.5)cm from underarm. Fasten off.

FINISHING
Collar
With I, beginning at right front neck edge, join yarn with sl st, ready to work across bottom edge of sts.
Row 1 (RS) Ch 3, 2 dc in first ch-sp, *sc into next sc, ch 3, 3 dc into next ch-3 sp; rep from * to last st, sc in last sc—34 (36, 36) pat reps.
Foll reverse Stripe Sequence, work even in pat for 8 rows. Fasten off.

Buttonbands
Join I at bottom edge of right front.
Row 1 (RS) Ch 3, 2 dc in same row end, *sc into next row end, ch 3, 3 dc into next row end; rep from * 4 more times, sc into next row end, ch 12, 3 dc into next row end**; rep from * to ** to last row of top of collar, sc in last row end. Fasten off—6 (7, 7) ch-12 lps. Join I at top edge of collar on left front.
Row 1 (RS) Ch 3, 2 dc in same row end, *sc into next row end, ch 3, 3 dc into next row end; rep from * to last row on bottom edge, sc in last row end. Fasten off.
Cut 5 (6, 6) 1"/2.5cm circles from felt piece. On left front, mark to line up with corresponding bottom 5 (6, 6) ch-12 lps on right front and attach to left front 4"/10cm away from edge.
Cut smaller felt circle a little less than ½"/1cm and attach to left front 4"/10cm away from edge, lining up with topmost ch-12 lp.
Sew smallest button to smallest felt circle. Sew remaining buttons to larger felt circles.
Sew sleeve seams. Block to measurements.•

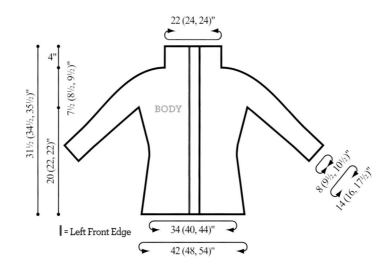

I = Left Front Edge

CARDI SHAWL

This cardi shawl by Jennifer Hansen, crocheted in a wavy-stitch pattern, is worked in a large rectangle that is folded and joined in three places to shape. A textured border is added in finishing.

●●●●
COMPLEX

SIZE
Sized for Small, Medium, Large, 1X, 2X, 3X and shown in size Small.

FINISHED MEASUREMENTS
• Bust 34¾ (37, 39¼, 43¾, 48¼, 52¾)"/88.5 (94, 99.5, 99, 111, 122.5, 134)cm
• Length 28¾ (29¾, 30¾, 33, 35¼, 37¾)"/72.5 (75.5, 77, 78.5, 84, 90, 95.5)cm
• Upper arm 13 (13, 14¾, 14¾, 16½, 16½)"/33 (33, 37.5, 37.5, 42, 42)cm

MATERIALS
• 10 (11, 12, 14, 16, 17) 1¾oz/50g hanks (each approx 186yd/173m) of Berroco *Flicker* (baby alpaca/acrylic/other fibers) in #3322 Pyotr (4)
• Size I/9 (5.5mm) hook *OR SIZE TO OBTAIN GAUGE*
• Stitch markers
• Yarn needle
• Rustproof pins
• Spray bottle

GAUGE
19 sts = 4"/10cm and 16 rows = 4½"/11.5cm over lacy wave stitch pat using size I/9 (5.5mm) hook.
TAKE TIME TO CHECK GAUGE.

NOTE
Cardi is worked in one rectangle, then seamed to create cardigan shape. Piece can be worn as shown or upside down with lower back as collar.

STITCH GLOSSARY
dtrtbl Double treble crochet in the back loop.
sctbl Single crochet in the back loop.
bpsc Back post single crochet.
bpdc Back post double crochet.

PATTERN
Ch 322 (322, 354, 354, 386, 386).
Row 1 (RS) Sc in 2nd ch from hook, sc in each ch across, turn—321, 321, 353, 353, 385, 385 sc.
Row 2 Ch 4 (counts as first st), sk first sc, *tr in the next sc, ch 1, sk next sc, dc in next sc, ch 1, sk next sc, hdc in next sc, ch 1, sk next sc, sc in each of the next 3 sc, ch 1, sk next sc, hdc in the next sc, ch 1, sk next sc, dc in the next sc, ch 1, sk next st, tr in the

next sc**, ch 1, sk next st; rep from * across stopping last rep at **, tr in the last st, turn.
Row 3 Ch 1, sctbl in each st across, turn.
Row 4 Ch 1, sc in the first st, *sc in the next st, ch 1, sk next st, hdc in the next st, ch 1, sk next sc, dc in the next st, ch 1, sk next st, [tr in the next sc, ch 1, sk next st] twice, dc in next sc, ch 1, sk next sc, hdc in next sc, ch 1, sk next sc, sc in each of the next 2 sc; rep from * across, turn.
Row 5 Rep row 3.
Rep rows 2–5 for 14 (15, 16, 18, 20, 22) times, fasten off.
Block to schematic size by pinning to size and spraying with water. Allow to dry before continuing.

Joining
Place stitch marker at following chs on foundation chain:
G: 27th (27th, 27th, 27th, 27th, 27th) st
F: 63rd (63rd, 67th, 67th, 71st, 71st) st
E: 125th (125th, 137th, 137th, 149th, 149th) st
D: 161st (161st, 177th, 177th, 193rd , 193rd) st
C: 197th (197th, 217th, 217th, 237th, 237th) st
B: 259th (259th, 287th, 287th, 315th, 315th) st
A: 295th (295th, 327th, 327th, 359th, 359th) st
Seam upper back (RS) With RS facing, to pin the following sts together: 1) B to C, 2) E to F, 3) A to D to G. Attach yarn with sl st through st at B, ch 3 (counts as first dc), dc in. Cont alternating sides working [sk next st, dc in the next st]. Dc in A, dc in D, dc in G to join all 3 portions of the back together. Dc in st AFTER D, dc in st AFTER G, then cont alternating along the upper back and left side of the piece until right armhole sts (E and F) are joined together. Fasten off.
Seam lower back (RS) Alternate stitch height with height of sts being joined. With RS facing, attach yarn with sl st to top of dc worked in D. Ch 3, dtr in the st AFTER A st, dtr in st AFTER G st, then cont alternating sides as foll: [sk 1 st, dtr in next st, (sk 1 st, dtr in next st on opposite side), sk 1 st, tr in next st, (sk 1 st, tr in next st on opposite side), sk 1 st, dc in next st, (sk 1 st, dc in next st on opposite side), {sk 1 st, hdc in next st, (sk 1 st, hdc in next st on opposite side)} twice, sk 1 st, dc in next st, (sk 1 st, dc in next st on opposite side), sk 1 st, tr in next st, (sk 1 st, tr in next st on opposite side), sk 1 st, dtr in next st, (sk 1 st, dtr in next st on opposite side)] twice, stopping 2nd rep after first hdc rep.
Work alternate hdcs in 2 rem sts. Fasten off.

Edging
With RS facing, attach yarn with sl st near the middle back of the cardigan.

Rnd 1 Ch 1, *sc in each sc across to corner, 3 sc in corner; rep from * around, sc in each sc to end, sl st to first sc, do not turn.

Rnd 2 Ch 5 (counts as dtr), *dtrtbl in each sc to corner, 5 dtrtbl in corner sc; rep from * around, dtrtbl in each sc to end, sl st to top of t-ch, do not turn.

Rnd 3 Ch 1, bpsc around t-ch, *bpsc in each dtr to corner, [ch 1, bpsc in next dtr] 4 times in corner; rep from * around, bpsc in each dtr to end, sl st to first sc, do not turn.

Rnd 4 Ch 4 (counts as dc, ch-1 sp), sk 1 sc, dc in next sc, *[ch 1, sk in next sc, dc in next sc] across to corner, [ch 2, dc in next sc] 4 times; rep from * around, [ch 1, sk in next sc, dc in next sc] across to end, ch 1, sl st to 3rd ch of t-ch, do not turn.

Rnd 5 Ch 1, bpsc around t-ch, *[ch 1, bpsc around next dc] across to corner, [ch 3, bpsc around next dc] 4 times; rep from * around, [ch 1, bpsc around next dc] across to end, ch 1, sl st to first sc, do not turn.

Rnd 6 Ch 5 (counts as first dtr), *dtr in each sc and ch-1 sp to corner, [3 dtr in ch-3 sp, dtr in next sc] 4 times; rep from * around, dtr in each sc and ch-1 sp to end, sl st to top of t-ch, do not turn.

Rnd 7 Ch 1, bpsc around t-ch, ch 2 (counts as first dc), *[ch 1, sk next dtr, bpdc around next dtr] across to corner, [ch 2, sk 1 dtr, bpdc around next dtr] 8 times; rep from * around, [ch 1, sk next dtr, bpdc around next dtr] around, ch 1, sl st to top of t-ch, fasten off and weave in ends.•

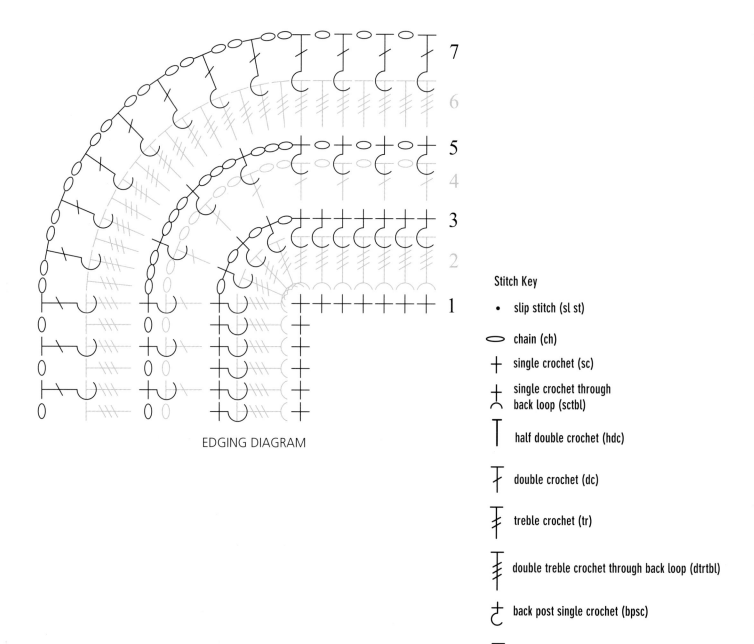

EDGING DIAGRAM

Stitch Key

• slip stitch (sl st)

◯ chain (ch)

+ single crochet (sc)

+ single crochet through back loop (sctbl)

| half double crochet (hdc)

| double crochet (dc)

| treble crochet (tr)

| double treble crochet through back loop (dtrtbl)

| back post single crochet (bpsc)

| back post double crochet (bpdc)

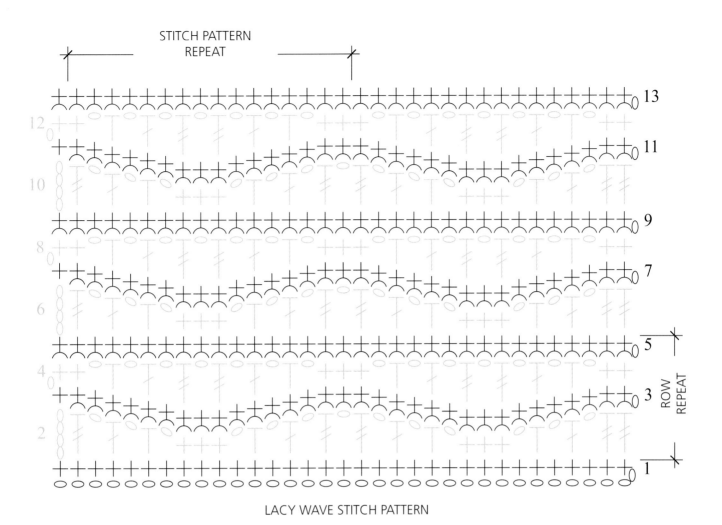

STITCH PATTERN
REPEAT

13

12
11

10

9

8
7

6

5

4
3 ROW REPEAT

2

1

LACY WAVE STITCH PATTERN

G   A

LOWER BACK JOINING DIAGRAM

Stitch Key

- • slip stitch (sl st)

- ⬯ chain (ch)

- + single crochet (sc)

- single crochet through back loop (sctbl)

- half double crochet (hdc)

- double crochet (dc)

- treble crochet (tr)

- double treble crochet through back loop (dtrtbl)

- back post single crochet (bpsc)

- back post double crochet (bpdc)

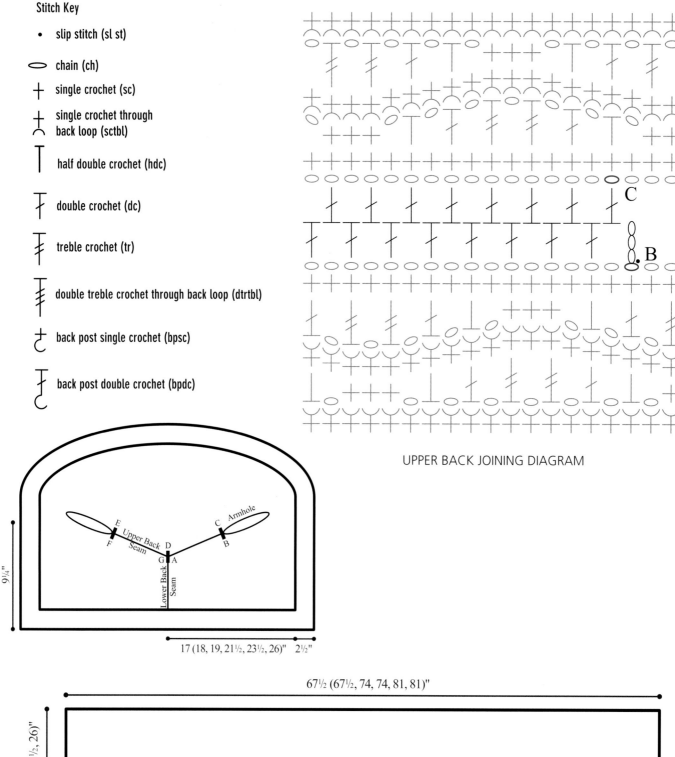

UPPER BACK JOINING DIAGRAM

9¼"

17 (18, 19, 21½, 23½, 26)"   2½"

67½ (67½, 74, 74, 81, 81)"

17 (18, 19, 21½, 23½, 26)"

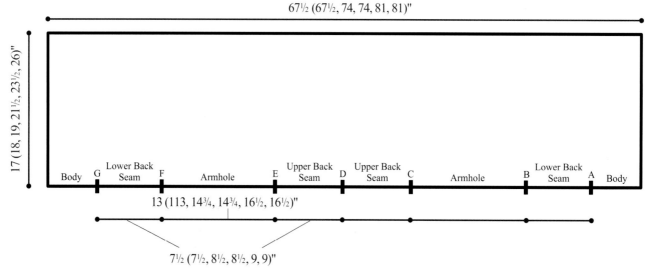

13 (113, 14¾, 14¾, 16½, 16½)"

7½ (7½, 8½, 8½, 9, 9)"

BUTTONED COWL

A crash course in elemental crochet techniques, Cristina Mershon's tailored neck warmer sports a classic feather-and-fan stitch. The button band gets its texture from single crochet worked through the back loop.

••
EASY

SIZE
Instructions are written for one size.

FINISHED MEASUREMENTS
Approx 11 x 24"/28 x 61cm

MATERIALS
• 1 3½oz/100g hank (each approx 400yd/366m) of Mountain Colors *Bearfoot* (superwash wool/mohair/nylon) each in burgundy (A), marigold (B), copper (C), raven (D) 🔳
• Size E/4 (3.5mm) crochet hook *OR SIZE TO OBTAIN GAUGE*
• Four ½"/13mm buttons
• Yarn needle, rustproof pins, spray bottle

GAUGE
20 sts and 11 rows = 4"/10cm over feather and fan pat using size E/4 (3.5mm) hook.
TAKE TIME TO CHECK GAUGE.

STITCH GLOSSARY
dctbl Double crochet in the back loop.
sctfl Single crochet in the front loop.
sctbl Single crochet in the back loop.

STRIPE PATTERN
Change color at end of each even row throughout in following sequence: A, B, C, D, A, C, B, A, D, C, B, A, D, C, A.

FEATHER AND FAN PATTERN
(ch 38 for gauge swatch)
Work following text below or chart pat.

COWL
Ch 110 with A. Work in feather and fan pat as foll:
Row 1 (RS) 4 dc in 4th ch from hook (sk ch count as dc), sk 1 ch, *dc in next ch, [sk 1 ch, dc in next ch] 6 times, sk 2 ch, 11 dc in next ch, sk 2 ch; rep from * 4 more times, [dc in next ch, sk 1 ch] 7 times, 5 dc in last ch, turn—107 dc.
Row 2 Ch 1, sctfl in each dc across, sc in top of t-ch, fasten off color, join new color, turn.
Row 3 Ch 3 (counts as dc), 4 dctbl in first sc, sk 1 sc, *dctbl in next sc, [sk 1 sc, dctbl in next sc] 6 times, sk 2 sc, 11 dctbl in next sc, sk 2 sc; rep from * 4 more times, [dctbl in next sc, sk 1 sc] 7 times, 5 dctbl in last sc, turn.
Rep rows 2 and 3 for 13 times more, rep row 2 once, fasten off.

FINISHING
Pin cowl to 11 x 21"/28 x 53.5cm. Spray with water and allow to dry.

Left edging (button side)
Join B with sl st to RS of left edge of cowl.
Row 1 Ch 1, sc evenly across edge (working in row ends), turn.
Row 2 Ch 1, sctbl in each sc across, turn.
Rep row 2 for 11 rows more, fasten off, weave in ends.

Right edging (buttonhole side)
Join B with sl st to RS of right edge of cowl.
Row 1 Ch 1, sc evenly across edge (working in row ends), turn.
Row 2 Ch 1, sctbl in each sc across, turn.
Rep row 2 for 4 rows more.
Row 7 Ch 1, sctbl in each sc across to last 26 sc, *ch 3, sk 3 sc, sctbl in next 3 sc; rep from * 3 more times, sctbl in each sc across to end, turn—4 buttonholes made.
Row 8 Ch 1, sctbl in each sc across, 3 sc in each ch-3 sp across, turn.
Rep row 2 for 5 times more, fasten off.
Sew buttons to left edging opposite buttonholes on right edging.•

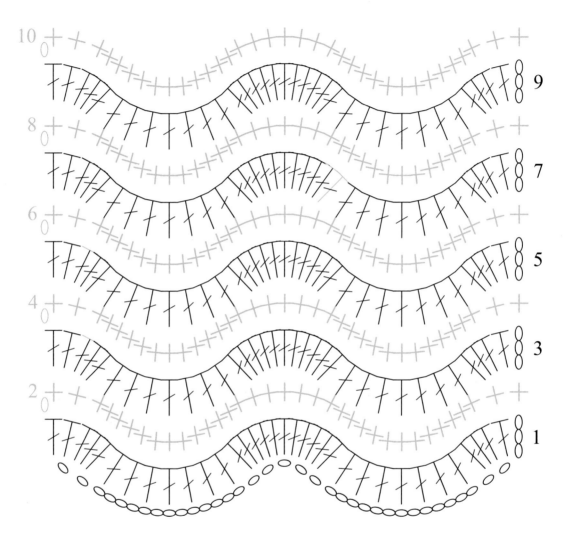

FEATHER AND FAN STITCH PATTERN

Stitch Key

⬯ chain (ch)

✝ single crochet in front loop (sctfl)

Ŧ double crochet (dc)

GRANNY SQUARE THROW

Using the traditional granny square as his canvas, Kaffe Fassett envisions a joyous palette, using more than a dozen colors. The squares are crocheted separately in the round using a different color for each round. A visible slip stitch joins the squares; a shell pattern finishes the outer border.

••
EASY

FINISHED MEASUREMENTS
44 x 50½"/112 x 128.5cm

MATERIALS
• 1 3½oz/100g hank (each approx 219yd/200m) of Rowan *Creative Linen* (linen/cotton) in #638 eggplant (A), #631 raspberry (B), #624 foggy (E-light gray), #628 ochre (F), #627 salmon (J), #622 straw (M), #625 teal (N), #626 lilac (O), and #636 darkness (P-teal) (4)
• 2 hanks in #632 leaf (C), #630 denim (D), #633 carin (H-red), and #637 coleus (K-burgundy)
• 2 1¾oz/50g skeins (each approx 93yd/85m) of Rowan *Handknit Cotton* (cotton) in #303 sugar (G-pink), #357 yacht (L), #365 blue john (Q) (4)
• 3 skeins in #250 florence (I-orange)
• Crochet hook size 7 (4.5mm) *OR SIZE TO OBTAIN GAUGE*

GAUGE
1 granny square = approx 6½"/16.5cm using size 7 (4.5mm) crochet hook.
TAKE TIME TO CHECK GAUGE.

GRANNY SQUARE
With first color, ch 4. Join ch with a sl st forming a ring.
Rnd 1 (RS) Ch 3 (always counts as 1 dc), work 2 dc in ring, ch 2, [work 3 dc in ring, ch 2] 3 times. Join rnd with a sl st in top of beg ch-3. Fasten off. From RS, join second color with a sl st in any corner ch-2sp.
Rnd 2 Ch 3, work 2 dc in same ch-2 sp, ch 1, [work (3 dc, ch 2, 3 dc) in next ch-2 sp, ch 1] 3 times, end work 3 dc in beg ch-2 sp, ch 2. Join rnd with sl st in top of beg ch-3. Fasten off. From RS, join third color with sl st in any corner ch-2 sp.
Rnd 3 Ch 3, work 2 dc in same ch-2 sp, ch 1, [work 3 dc in next ch-1 sp, ch 1, work (3 dc, ch 2, 3 dc) in next ch-2 sp, ch 1] 3 times, end work 3 dc in next ch-1 sp, ch 1, work 3 dc in beg ch-2 sp, ch 2. Join rnd with sl st in top of beg ch-3. Fasten off. From RS, join fourth color with sl st in any corner ch-2 sp.
Rnd 4 Ch 3, work 2 dc in same ch-2 sp, ch 1, *[work 3 dc in next ch-1 sp, ch 1] twice, work (3 dc, ch 2, 3 dc) in next ch-2 sp, ch 1; rep from * 3 times, end [work 3 dc in next ch-1 sp, ch 1] twice, work 3 dc in beg ch-2 sp, ch 2. join rnd with sl st in top of beg ch-3. Fasten off. From RS, join fifth color with sl st in any corner ch-2 sp.
Rnd 5 Ch 3 and cont in pat as established, working one more (3 dc, ch 1) between corners and working (3 dc, ch 2, 3 dc) in each corner. Fasten off. From RS, join sixth color with sl st in any corner ch-2 sp.

Rnd 6 Rep rnd 5. Fasten off. From RS, join seventh color with sl st in any corner ch-2 sp.
Rnd 7 Rep rnd 5. Fasten off. From RS, join H with a sl st in any corner ch-2 sp.
Rnd 8 With H Rep rnd 5. Fasten off.

THROW
Make 42 granny squares using designated color sequences. Unless noted, make one square of each color sequence.

SQUARE 1
Color sequence A, B, C, D, E, F, G

SQUARE 2
Color sequence I, C, J, D, E, K, F

SQUARE 3
Color sequence L, M, N, K, J, O, P

SQUARE 4
Color sequence G, F, E, D, C, B, A

SQUARE 5 (Make 2)
Color sequence P, C, I, K, L, Q, I

SQUARE 6 (Make 2)
Color sequence D, G, O, I, J, L, K

SQUARE 7
Color sequence P, B, A, O, C, J, B

SQUARE 8
Color sequence K, L, J, I, O, G, D

SQUARE 9
Color sequence A, B, J, C, P, F, A

SQUARE 10 (Make 2)
Color sequence Q, O, L, A, B, O, J

SQUARE 11
Color sequence F, K, E, D, J, C, I

SQUARE 12 (Make 2)
Color sequence I, Q, L, K, I, C, P

SQUARE 13
Color sequence O, K, F, J, K, D, O

SQUARE 14
Color sequence A, J, C, E, N, P, Q

SQUARE 15
Color sequence Q, P, N, E, C, J, A

SQUARE 16
Color sequence G, I, J, B, O, K, A

SQUARE 17
Color sequence E, C, Q, L, P, K, I

SQUARE 18 (Make 2)
Color sequence P, O, J, K, N, M, L

SQUARE 19 (Make 2)
Color sequence F, G, J, D, Q, C, K

SQUARE 20
Color sequence B, O, K, F, Q, C, A

SQUARE 21 (Make 2)
Color sequence A, K, O, B, J, I, G

SQUARE 22 (Make 2)
Color sequence J, O, B, A, L, O, Q

SQUARE 23
Color sequence L, D, M, B, C, A, M

SQUARE 24
Color sequence E, C, Q, L, P, K, I

SQUARE 25
Color sequence A, C, Q, F, K, O, B

SQUARE 26
Color sequence O, D, K, J, F, K, O

SQUARE 27
Color sequence K, C, Q, D, J, G, F

SQUARE 28
Color sequence A, F, P, C, J, B, A

SQUARE 29
Color sequence J, D, O, F, P, C, F

SQUARE 30
Color sequence B, J, C, O, A, B, P

SQUARE 31
Color sequence M, A, C, B, M, D, L

SQUARE 32
Color sequence I, K, P, L, Q, C, E

SQUARE 33
Color sequence F, C, P, F, O, D, J

SQUARE 34
Color sequence G, F, E, D, C, B, A •

FINISHING
Using diagram and A, sc granny squares tog so that the sc shows on the RS.

Edging
Rnd 1 Join D in any corner ch-2 sp, Ch 3, work 2 dc in same ch-2 sp, ch 1, *work (3 dc, ch 1) in each ch-1 and ch-2 sp along one edge of afghan to next corner, work (3 dc, ch 2, 3 dc) in corner ch-2 sp; rep from * around all 4 edges, end with work 3 dc in beg ch-2 sp, ch 2. Join rnd with sl st in top of beg ch-3. Fasten off. From RS, join K to any corner ch-2 sp.
Rep rnd 1, changing to C at end of rnd.
Rep rnd 1, changing to I at end of rnd.
Rep rnd 1, changing to H at end of rnd.
Last rnd Ch 3, work 1 dc in same ch-2 sp as joining, *ch 1, sc in next ch-2 sp, ch 1, (2 dc, ch 2, 2 dc) in next ch-2 sp; rep from * around entire afghan, end with 2 dc, ch 2 in beg ch sp.
Fasten off. •

ASSEMBLY DIAGRAM

1	2	3	4	5	6
7	8	9	10	11	12
13	14	15	16	17	18
19	20	12	18	21	22
23	24	25	5	26	21
27	6	28	29	22	30
31	32	33	10	34	19

BOATNECK PULLOVER

Allover open shell-stitch patterning creates a polka-dot effect on Deborah Newton's boatneck pullover. Drop shoulders and an oversized fit enhance the swingy trapeze silhouette; narrow three-quarter sleeves add a trim note.

●●●
INTERMEDIATE

SIZE
Sized for X-Small/Small, Medium/Large, 1X/2X and shown in size X-Small/Small.

FINISHED MEASUREMENTS
• Bust 50 (55, 60)"/127 (139.5, 152.5)cm
• Length 26½ (28, 30)"/67 (71, 76)cm
• Upper arm 14 (15½, 17)"/35.5 (39, 43)cm

MATERIALS
• 4 (5, 5) 3½oz/100g skeins (each approx 437yd/400m) of Cascade Yarns *Heritage Silk* (wool/silk) in #5630 aqua foam ❶
• Size F/5 (3.75mm) crochet hook *OR SIZE TO OBTAIN GAUGE*
• Tapestry needle

GAUGE
4 shells = 5"/12.5cm and 9 rows = 4"/10cm over pat st using size F/5 (3.75mm) hook.
TAKE TIME TO CHECK GAUGE.

NOTES
1 Pattern is worked over a multiple of 6 sts plus 4.
2 Seams may affect finished size; work loosely to avoid pulling.

BACK
Ch 124 (136, 148).
Setup row (WS) 2 dc in 4th ch from hook, *ch 4, sk 5 ch, 5 dc in next ch; rep from * to last ch, 3 dc in last ch. Ch 1, turn—20 (22, 24) ch-4 spaces.
Pat row 1 (RS) *(3 dc, ch 3, 3 dc) in next ch-4 sp; rep from *, end sc in top of t-ch. Ch 6, turn—20 (22, 24) shells.
Pat row 2 (WS) *5 dc in next ch-3 sp, ch 4; rep from *, end ch 3, dc in t-ch. Ch 5, turn.
Pat row 3 3 dc in ch-3 sp, *(3 dc, ch 3, 3 dc) in next ch-4 sp; rep from * to t-ch, (3 dc, ch 2, dc) in t-ch sp. Ch 3, turn.
Pat row 4 2 dc in ch-2 sp, *ch 4, 5 dc in next ch-3 sp; rep from *, end ch 4, 3 dc in t-ch sp. Ch 1, turn.
Rep pat rows 1–4 for 13 (14, 15) times more, ending with a row 4.

Shoulder and neck shaping
Next row (RS) *(3 dc, ch 3, 3 dc) in next ch-4 sp; rep from * 5 (6, 6) times more. Ch 6, turn, leaving rem sts unworked—6 (7, 7) shells.
Next row (WS) *5 dc in next ch-3 sp, ch 4; rep from *

2 (2, 3) more times, 3 dc in next ch-3 sp. Ch 5, turn, leaving rem sts unworked.
Next row (RS) 3 dc in next ch-4 sp, *(3 dc, ch 3, 3 dc) in next ch-4 sp; rep from *, end 3 dc in t-ch sp. Fasten off.
With RS facing, skip center 8 (8, 10) shells. Join yarn in next ch-4 sp and cont pat over last 6 (7, 7) shells. Complete to correspond to first shoulder, reversing shaping.

FRONT
Work same as Back.

SLEEVES
Ch 52 (58, 64).
Setup row (WS) 2 dc in 4th ch from hook, *ch 4, sk 5 ch, 5 dc in next ch; rep from * to last ch, 3 dc in last ch. Ch 1, turn—8 (9, 10) ch-4 spaces.
Pat row 1 (RS) *(3 dc, ch 3, 3 dc) in next ch-4 sp; rep from *, end sc in top of t-ch. Ch 6, turn—8 (9, 10) shells.
Pat row 2 (WS) *5 dc in next ch-3 sp, ch 4; rep from *, end ch 3, dc in t-ch. Ch 5, turn.
Pat row 3 3 dc in ch-3 sp, *(3 dc, ch 3, 3 dc) in next ch-4 sp; rep from * to t-ch, (3 dc, ch 2, dc) in t-ch sp. Ch 3, turn.
Pat row 4 2 dc in ch-2 sp, *ch 4, 5 dc in next ch-3 sp; rep from *, end ch 4, 3 dc in t-ch sp. Ch 1, turn.
Rep pat rows 1–4 six times more, ending with a row 4. Do not ch at end of final row 4.
Inc row (RS) Ch 7, 2 dc in 4th ch from hook, ch 3, *(3 dc, ch 3, 3 dc) in next ch-4 sp; rep from * across, ch 3, 3 dc into t-ch. Ch 6, turn—10 (11, 12) ch-3 spaces.
Work pat rows 2–4 as established.

Sizes XS/S only
Rep inc row—12 ch-3 spaces.

Sizes M/L, 1X/2X only
Rep inc row—(13, 14) ch-3 spaces. Work (1, 2) more rows in pat. Fasten off.

FINISHING
Block pieces to measurements. Sew shoulder seams. Place markers 7 (7¾, 8½)"/18 (19.5, 21.5)cm from shoulder seam on front and back. Sew top of sleeve to front and back between markers.

Neckline trim
With RS facing, join yarn at shoulder seam.

Rnd 1 (RS) Ch 3, dc evenly spaced around neck edge, join with sl st in top of t-ch. Do not turn.
Rnd 2 Ch 1, sc in each dc around, join with sl st in first sc. Do not turn.
Rnd 3 Ch 3, dc in next sc and in each sc around, join with sl st in t-ch. Fasten off. Sew side and sleeve seams.

Sleeves lower edge trim
With RS facing, join yarn at sleeve seam at lower edge of sleeve.

Rnd 1 (RS) Ch 3, *4 dc in next ch-sp, sk 2 dc, dc between last skipped dc and next dc, sk 1 dc, dc between last skipped dc and next dc; rep from * around, sl st in top of t-ch. Fasten off.

Body lower edge trim
With RS facing, join yarn at side seam at bottom edge of body. Work as for sleeves lower edge trim.•

SHELL-STITCH PATTERN

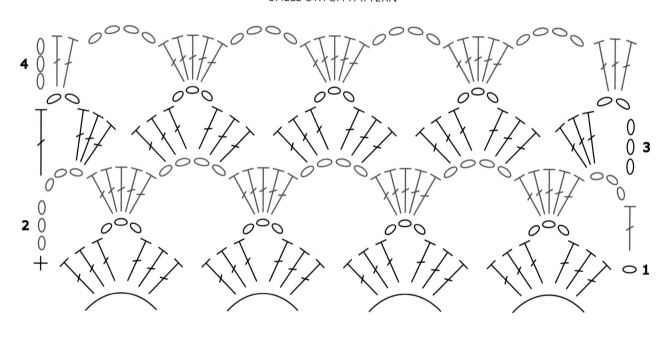

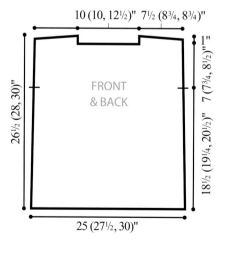

FRONT & BACK

10 (10, 12½)" 7½ (8¾, 8¾)"

26½ (28, 30)"

18½ (19¼, 20½)" 7 (7¾, 8½)"

1"

25 (27½, 30)"

Stitch Key
⬯ chain (ch)
+ single crochet (sc)
⊤ double crochet (dc)

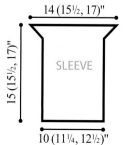

14 (15½, 17)"

SLEEVE

15 (15½, 17)"

10 (11¼, 12½)"

122

SHELL-STITCH BAG

Yoko Hatta creates tons of visual interest on her boho bag by striping a simple shell-stitch pattern with three shades of yarn. Single crochet creates a casing for the purchased handles.

INTERMEDIATE

FINISHED MEASUREMENTS
Bag is 21 x 12½"/53.5 x 32cm

MATERIALS
• 3 1¾oz/50g hanks (each approx 98yd/90m) of Fibre Company/Kelbourne Woolens *Organik* (wool/baby alpaca/silk) each in coral reef (A), loam (B), magma (C) (4)
• Size E/4 (3.5mm) hook *OR SIZE TO OBTAIN GAUGE*
• Two 5"/13cm diameter handles
• Yarn needle, rustproof pins, spray bottle

GAUGE
3 shs = 5"/13cm and 10 rows = 4"/10cm over coral shell-stitch pat #1 using size E/4 (3.5mm) hook.
TAKE TIME TO CHECK GAUGE.

COLOR SEQUENCE
Change color at end of each row throughout as foll: A, B, C.

NOTES
Bag is worked from the foundation chain to the handles, then yarn is attached at the foundation chain and worked on the opposite side up to the handles.

STITCH GLOSSARY
Large shell (lg sh) 7 dc in same st.
Small shell (sm sh) 5 dc in same st.
sctbl Single crochet in the back loop.

FIRST HALF
With A, ch 122.
Follow text below or chart.
Row 1 (RS) Sc in 2nd ch from hook, *sk 3 ch, lg sh in next ch, sk 3 ch, sc in next ch; rep from * across, change color, turn—15 shells.
Row 2 (st pat #1) Ch 3 (counts as dc), 3 dc in first sc, *sk 3 dc, sc in next dc, lg sh in next sc; rep from * to last sh, sk 3 dc, sc in next dc, 4 dc in last sc, change color, turn.
Row 3 Ch 1, sc in first dc, *lg sh in next sc, sk 3 dc, sc in next dc; rep from * across, sc in top of t-ch, change color, turn.
Rep rows 2 and 3 four times more. Rep row 2 once.
Row 13 Ch 1, sc in first dc, *sm sh in next sc, sk 3 dc, sc in next dc; rep from * across, sc in top of t-ch, change color, turn.
Row 14 (st pat #2) Ch 3 (counts as dc), 2 dc in first sc, *sk 2 dc, sc in next dc, sm sh in next sc; rep from * to last sh, sk 2 dc, sc in next dc, 3 dc in last sc, change color, turn.
Row 15 Ch 1, sc in first dc, *sm sh in next sc, sk 2 dc, sc in next

dc; rep from * across, sc in top of t-ch, change color, turn.
Rep rows 14 and 15 twice. Rep row 14 once.
Row 21 Ch 1, sc in first dc, *3 dc in next sc, sk 2 dc, sc in next dc; rep from * across, sc in top of t-ch, change color, turn.
Row 22 (st pat #3) Ch 3 (counts as dc), dc in first sc, *sk 1 dc, sc in next dc, 3 dc in next sc; rep from * to last sh, sk 1 dc, sc in next dc, 2 dc in last sc, change color, turn.
Row 23 Ch 1, sc in first dc, *3 dc in next sc, sk 1 dc, sc in next dc; rep from * across, sc in top of t-ch, change color, turn.
Rep rows 22 and 23 three times. Rep row 22 once.
Row 31 With A, ch 1, sc in first st, sc in next st, [sc2tog over next 2 sts] 10 times, sc in next st, [sc2tog over next 2 sts] 4 times, sc in next st, [sc2tog over next 2 sts] 3 times, sc in next st, [sc2tog over next 2 sts] 10 times, sc in last 2 sts, turn.
Row 32 Ch 1, sctbl in each sc across, turn.
Rep row 32 six times more, fasten off.

SECOND HALF

Join A on RS of foundation chain with sl st, rep row 1. Complete as for first half.

FINISHING

Pin bag out to schematic size, spray with water, and allow to dry.

Edging

Row 1 Join A to side of handle cover on RS. Ch 1, sc 6 times down handle cover section (working in ends of rows), sc 40 times across side of bag to other handle cover section (working in ends of rows, gathering the side as you go), sc 6 times to end, working in ends of rows, turn.

Row 2 Ch 1, sctbl in each sc across, turn.

Rep row 2 twice, fasten off.

Rep on opposite side of bag.

Place handle inside handle cover and pin. Whipstitch in place. Rep for other handle. •

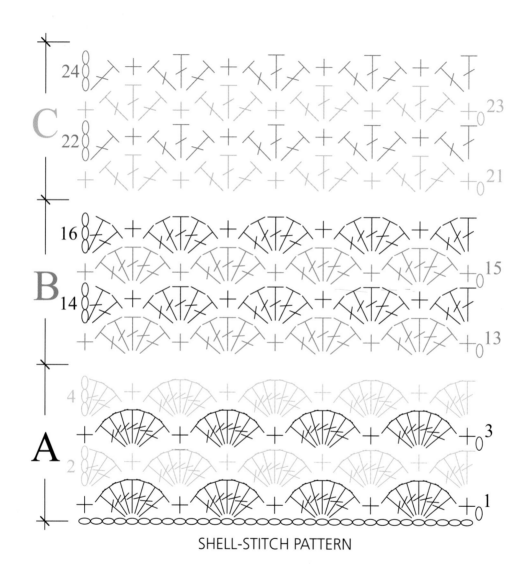

SHELL-STITCH PATTERN

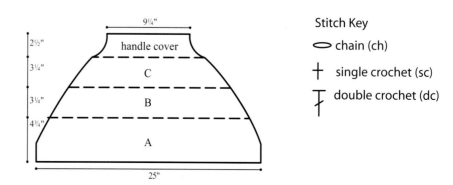

Stitch Key

⬭ chain (ch)

+ single crochet (sc)

T double crochet (dc)

RIBBON NECKLACE

For her boho-chic ribbon necklace, Yoko Hatta flanks a single solid-colored rose with a succession of two-toned daisies, all secured to a crocheted chain-loop strand. A length of grosgrain ribbon loops around the end of the chain and ties at the back.

●●●
INTERMEDIATE

SIZE
Instructions are written for one size.

FINISHED MEASUREMENTS
• Length of chain 10"/25.5cm

MATERIALS
• 1 2.8oz/80g ball (each approx 400yd/366m) of Aunt Lydia's *Crochet Thread Classic 10* (mercerized cotton) each in #423 maize (A), #479 bridal blue (B), and #210 antique white (C) (10)
• Size 7 steel (1.5mm) crochet hook
• One size 7 (4.5mm) knitting needle for making flower centers
• 2 yd/m of ½"/15mm grosgrain ribbon

GAUGE
Gauge is not important for this project.

CHAIN
With C, ch 99, join with sl st in 9th ch from hook for end lp, *ch 4, sk 4 ch, sl st in next ch; rep from * to last ch, ch 8, join with sl st in last ch for end lp.
Rnd 1 Ch 1, [*5 sc in next ch-4 sp; rep from * to end lp, 12 sc in end lp] twice, join with sl st to ch 1. Fasten off.

FLOWER MOTIF
With A, make 1.
Ch 6. Join ch with a sl st to first ch to form a ring.
Rnd 1 (RS) Ch 1, work 12 sc in ring, join with sl st to ch 1.
Rnd 2 (RS) Ch 1, sc in next sc, *ch 3, sk 1 sc, sc in next sc; rep from * 4 times more, ch 3, join with sl st to ch 1.
Rnd 3 (RS) Ch 1, *(sc, hdc, 3 dc, hdc, sc) in ch-3 sp; rep from * 5 times more, join with sl st to ch 1, turn.
Rnd 4 (WS) BPsc around sc of rnd 2, *ch 5, BPsc around sc from rnd 2; rep from * 4 times, ch 5, join with sl to to BPsc, turn.
Rnd 5 (RS) Ch 1, *(sc, hdc, 5 dc, hdc, sc) in ch-5 sp; rep from * 5 times more, join with sl st to ch 1, turn.
Rnd 6 (WS) BPsc around BPsc of rnd 4, *ch 7, BPsc around BPsc from rnd 4; rep from * 4 times more, ch 7, join with sl st to BPsc, turn.
Rnd 7 (RS) Ch 1, *(sc, hdc, 7dc, hdc, sc) in ch-7 sp; rep from * 5 times more, join with sl st to ch 1. Fasten off.

DAISY MOTIF
With A and C, make 2. With B and C, make 4.
Note When changing colors, work last 2 lps of last st before change with new color.
With A or B, ch 4. Join ch with a sl st to first ch to form ring.
Rnd 1 (RS) Ch 1, work 8 sc in ring, join with a sl st to ch 1.
Petals *Ch 12, sc in 2nd ch from hook, hdc in next 2 ch, dc in next 4 ch, hdc in next 2 ch, sc in next 2 ch, join with sl st to next sc in ring; rep from * 7 times more, joining C on last st.
Petal edging With C, *sc in each ch along foundation ch, ch 1, sc2tog over next 2 sts, sc in each st to 1 st before ring, sc2tog last st of petal edge tog with first st of next petal edge; rep from * 7 times more, omitting sc2tog at base of final petal. Fasten off.

FLOWER CENTERS
Make 1 in A, 6 in C.
Wrap A or C around needle 8 times, remove from needle and work 16 sc into ring, join with a sl st to beg of rnd. Working over first rnd, work 14 sc into ring. Fasten off.

LEAF MOTIF
Make 2 in C.
Ch 15.
Row 1 Sc in 2nd ch from hook and in each of next 12 ch, 3 sc in last ch for leaf tip, cont along other side of ch, sc in each ch to 1 ch before end, turn—27 sc.
Row 2 Ch 1, sc in each sc to 1 st before tip, 3 sc in next sc, 1 sc in each sc to 2 scs before end, turn.
Rows 3–6 Rep row 2.
Fasten off.

FINISHING
Using photo as guide, arrange Flower Motif 1 and Flower Center in A on top of 2 Leaf Motifs at center of chain and sew in place. Arrange Daisy Motifs with Flower Centers in C on either side of center motif as foll: B, A, B. Sew in place.
Loop ribbon through end loops of chain and tie in back to wear.●

MITERED SHAWL

The classic crocheted shawl gets an update with Jane Slicer-Smith's mitered wrap that integrates three yarns. This wrap allows you to join the squares— worked in stripes of single crochet—as you go, alleviating the need for seaming.

●●●●
COMPLEX

SIZE
Instructions are written for one size.

FINISHED MEASUREMENTS
60"/152cm x 60"/152cm at widest/longest point

MATERIALS
- 6 .88 oz/25g balls (each approx 230yd/210m) of Trendsetter Yarns *Super Kid Seta* (mohair/silk) in #10 teal (A) **1**
- 7 balls in #1001 ecru (B)
- 5 1¾oz/50g hanks (each approx 110yd/100m) of Trendsetter Yarns *Acacia* (cotton/viscose/silk/hemp/linen) in #164 denim (C) **3**
- 6 1¾/50g hanks (each approx 75yd/69m) of Trendsetter Yarns *Zoe* (cotton/viscose/polyester) in #3 lilacs & clovers (D) **4**
- Size E/4 (3.5mm) and size G/6 (4mm) hook

OR SIZES TO OBTAIN GAUGE

GAUGE
20 sts and 16 rows = 4"/10cm over sc using larger hook and *Super Kid Seta*; each finished square = approx 5"/13cm.
TAKE TIME TO CHECK GAUGE.

Note To achieve gauge, use smaller hook when using *Acacia* or *Zoe*, use the larger hook when using *Super Kid Seta*.

STITCHING INSTRUCTIONS
1) After the first square of each piece, there are three different ways to stitch a mitered square. One builds the work out horizontally, one builds the work up vertically, and one fills in a preexisting hole. Use the stitching instructions below for the square you wish to make, and use the assembly diagram for color selection and placement.
2) Remember that the different yarns require different size crochet hooks.
3) Always work first row of sc in the back or bump of the chain for a neater finish.

SQUARES
First square
Ch 49.
Row 1 Sc in 2nd ch from hook (working in the back or bump of the ch) and in each of next 22 ch, sc2tog, sc in each sc to end— 47 sc, 23 on either side of a central decrease st. Ch 1, turn.
Row 2 Sc in each of first 22 sc, sc3tog, sc in each sc to end. Ch 1, turn—45 sc, 22 on either side of a central decrease st.

Row 3 Sc in each sc until 1 sc rems before decrease, sc3tog, sc in each sc to end. Ch 1, turn.
Rep row 3 until 3 sc rem. Each row will have 2 fewer sts than the row before.
Final row Sc3tog. Fasten off.

Square building out horizontally
Insert hook in the bottom right outside ch of the adjacent square. Ch 25.
Row 1 Sc in 2nd ch from hook (working in the back or bump of the ch) and in each of next 22 ch, sc2tog over the last ch of the ch-25 and the side of the first row of the adjacent square, work 23 more sc evenly spaced to top right corner of adjacent square. Ch 1, turn.
Rep instructions for first square from row 2 to end.

Square building up vertically
When stitching these squares, the opposite side of the work will be facing you from when you were working the horizontal squares. Don't worry about RS/WS on mitered square projects because the difference is not obvious.
Insert hook in the outside left top ch of the adjacent square. With specified color, ch 25.
Rep all instructions of square building out horizontally.

Square filling in a preexisting spot
Note Fill-in squares have 1 more sc on each side than exterior squares to help the piece lie flat.
Row 1 Starting with the outside edge (rightmost if you are right-handed, leftmost if you are left-handed), work 24 sc evenly spaced to corner, sc2tog placing one half of the st on the bottom edge and one half of the st on the side edge, work 24 more sc evenly spaced to top of side—49 sts, 24 sc on either side of a central decrease. Ch 1, turn.
Row 2 Sc in each of first 23 sc, sc3tog, sc in each sc to end— 47 sc, 23 on either side of a central decrease st. Ch 1, turn.
Rep instructions for first square from row 3 to end.

COLOR SEQUENCE
Block 1
Ch and rows 1 and 2 Work 1 strand each A and B held tog.
Rows 3 and 4 Color C.
Rows 5–12 Rep rows 1–4 twice more.
Rows 13 and 14 Work 2 strands of B held tog.
Rows 15 and 16 Color C.

Rows 17–20 Rep rows 13–16.
Rows 21 and 22 2 strands of B held tog.
Row 23 Color C.

Block 2
Ch and rows 1 and 2 Work 2 strands B held tog.
Rows 3 and 4 Color D.
Rows 5–12 Rep rows 1–4 twice more.
Rows 13 and 14 2 strands of A held tog.
Rows 15 and 16 2 strands of B held tog.
Rows 17–20 Rep row 13–16.
Rows 21 and 22 2 strands of A held tog.
Row 23 2 strands of B held tog.

Block 3
Ch and rows 1 and 2 Color C.
Rows 3 and 4 2 strands of A held tog.
Rows 5–12 Rep rows 1–4 twice more.
Rows 13 and 14 Color D.
Rows 15 and 16 2 strands of A held tog.
Rows 17–20 Rep rows 13–16.
Rows 21 and 22 Color D.
Row 23 2 strands of A held tog.

Block 4
Ch and rows 1 and 2 2 strands of A held tog.
Rows 3 and 4 Color C.
Rows 5–20 Rep rows 1–4 four times more.
Rows 21 and 22 1 strand each of A and B held tog.
Row 23 Color C.

Block 5
Ch and rows 1 and 2 Color D.
Rows 3 and 4 2 strands of B held tog.
Rows 5–8 Rep rows 1–4.
Rows 9 and 10 2 strands of A held tog.
Rows 11 and 12 2 strands of B held tog.
Rows 13–20 Rep rows 9–12 twice more.
Rows 21 and 22 2 strands of A held tog.
Row 23 2 strands of B held tog.

Block 6
Ch and rows 1 and 2 2 strands of A held tog.
Rows 3 and 4 1 strand each of A and B held tog.
Rows 5–20 Rep rows 1–4 four times more.
Rows 21 and 22 Color C.
Row 23 1 strand each of A and B held tog.

Block 7
Ch and rows 1 and 2 2 strands of A held tog.
Rows 3 and 4 Color C.
Rows 5–18 Rep rows 1–4 three times more, then rep rows 1 and 2 once more.
Rows 19 and 20 Color D.
Rows 21 and 22 2 strands of A held tog.
Row 23 Color D.

Block 8
Ch and rows 1 and 2 2 strands of B held tog.
Rows 3 and 4 1 strand each of A and B held tog.
Rows 5–12 Rep rows 1–4 twice more.
Rows 13 and 14 Color D.
Rows 15 and 16 1 strand each of A and B held tog.
Rows 17–20 Rep rows 13–16.
Rows 21 and 22 Color D.
Row 23 1 strand each of A and B held tog.

WRAP

Using diagram, match up instructions for the block you wish to make (building out horizontally, building up vertically, or filling in a preexisting square) with the color sequence (blocks 1–8 above). Wrap is made in two pieces as shown, to keep the block orientation consistent while minimizing finishing.
Crochet each piece beg with first square as noted in diagrams.

FINISHING

Match pieces at A and B on diagrams and sew tog. ●

ASSEMBLY DIAGRAM

			1	3	2	A
		6	4	5	4	6
	5	2	8	7	2	8
2	4	6	7	4	7	6
*1	3	5	1	3	5	8	B

DIAGRAM KEY

↗ = **Direction of work**
* = **First square**
Numeral indicates color block

A

1	3	8	7	1
4	5	6	2	7
3	8	1	6	8
7	2	8	5	3
1	7	3	4	1	B
8	6	8	6	2
5	7	2	4	3
3	4	7	5	1
1	7	8	4
5	6	2	6
3	4	5
*1	2

60"

PINEAPPLE-STITCH DOLMAN

Yoko Hatta's sweet yet saucy dolman top shows off a traditional pineaple stitch and pretty picot edging. It's crocheted in one piece from the neck down.

••
EASY

SIZE
Sized for X-Small/Small, Medium/Large and shown in size X-Small/Small.

FINISHED MEASUREMENTS
• Width at widest point approx 96 (100)"/244 (254)cm
• Waistband 33½ (39½)"/85 (100.5)cm
• Length approx 24 (25)"/61 (63.5)cm
• Forearm 9"/23cm

MATERIALS
• 10 (12) 1¾oz/50g balls (each approx 153yd/140m) of Rowan/Westminster Fibers *Siena 4 Ply* (cotton) in #682 shrimp (pink) **1**
• Size E/4 (3.5mm) hook *OR SIZE TO OBTAIN GAUGE*

GAUGE
21 sts and 16 rows = 4"/10cm over alternating rows dc and sc.
TAKE TIME TO CHECK GAUGE.

NOTES
If working from chart, read all rnds from right to left. The beg of each rnd is within the chart, not at the edge.

STITCH GLOSSARY
2-dc V Work (dc, ch 1, dc) in 1 sp.
3-dc V Work (dc, ch 1, dc, ch 1, dc) in 1 sp.

TOP
Ch 196 (220), join ch with sl st in first ch to form ring, being careful not to twist ch.
Rnd 1 (Dc, ch 1, dc) in 5th ch from hook, ch 3, sk 2 ch, sc in next ch, [ch 4, sk 1 ch, sc in next ch] 3 times, ch 3, sk 2 ch, *3-dc V in next ch, ch 3, sk 2 ch, sc in next ch, [ch 4, sk 1 ch, sc in next ch] 3 times, ch 3, sk 2 ch; rep from * 14 (16) times more—16 (18) pat reps. Join rnd with sl st in 3rd ch of beg ch-4 at end of this and every foll rnd.
Note This join will no longer be mentioned. Ch-1, ch-4, etc. denotes ch-1 sp, ch-4 sp, etc.
Rnd 2 Ch 4, dc in first ch-1, 2-dc V in next ch-1, ch 3, sc in next ch-4, [ch 4, sc in next ch-4] twice, ch 3, *[2-dc V in next ch-1] twice, ch 3, sc in next ch-4, [ch 4, sc in next ch-4] twice, ch 3; rep from * around.
Rnd 3 Ch 4, dc in first ch-1, ch 4, 2-dc V in next ch-1, ch 3, sc in next ch-4, ch 4, sc in next ch-4, ch 3, *2-dc V in next ch-1, ch 4, 2-dc V in next ch-1, ch 3, sc in next ch-4, ch 4, sc in next ch-4, ch 3; rep from * around.

Rnd 4 Ch 4, dc in first ch-1, ch 1, 5 dc in next ch-4, ch 1, 2-dc V in next ch-1, ch 3, sc in next ch-4, ch 3, *2-dc V in next ch-1, ch 1, 5 dc in next ch-4, ch 1, 2-dc V in next ch-1, ch 3, sc in next ch-4, ch 3; rep from * around.
Rnd 5 Ch 4, dc in first ch-1, ch 2, dc in next dc, [ch 1, dc in next dc] 4 times, ch 2, 2-dc V in ch-1 of next 2-dc V, *2-dc V in ch-1 of next 2-dc V, ch 2, dc in next dc, [ch 1, dc in next dc] 4 times, ch 2, 2-dc V in ch-1 of next 2-dc V; rep from * around.
Rnd 6 (Sl st, ch 4, dc) in first ch-1, ch 3, sc in next ch-1, [ch 4, sc in next ch-1] 3 times, ch 3, 2-dc V in next ch-1, *2-dc V in next ch-1, ch 3, sc in next ch-1, [ch 4, sc in next ch-1] 3 times, ch 3, 2-dc V in next ch-1; rep from * around.
Rnd 7 (Sl st, ch 4, dc) in first ch-1, ch 3, sc in next ch-4, [ch 4, sc in next ch-4] twice, ch 3, 2-dc V in next ch-1, ch 1, *2-dc V in next ch-1, ch 3, sc in next ch-4, [ch 4, sc in next ch-4] twice, ch 3, 2-dc V in next ch-1, ch 1; rep from * around.
Rnd 8 (Sl st, ch 4, dc) in first ch-1, ch 3, sc in next ch-4, ch 4, sc in next ch-4, ch 3, 2-dc V in next ch-1, ch 5, *2-dc V in next ch-1,

ch 3, sc in next ch-4, ch 4, sc in next ch-4, ch 3, 2-dc V in next ch-1, ch 5; rep from * around.

Rnd 9 (Sl st, ch 4, dc) in first ch-1, ch 3, sc in next ch-4, ch 3, 2-dc V in next ch-1, ch 1, 6 dc in next ch-5, ch 1, *2-dc V in next ch-1, ch 3, sc in next ch-4, ch 3, 2-dc V in next ch-1, ch 1, 6 dc in next ch-5, ch 1; rep from * around.

Rnd 10 (Sl st, ch 4, dc) in first ch-1, 3-dc V in next ch-1, ch 2, dc in next dc, [ch 1, dc in next dc] 5 times, ch 2, *[3-dc V in ch-1 of next 2-dc V] twice, ch 2, dc in next dc, [ch 1, dc in next dc] 5 times, ch 2; rep from * around, end dc in first ch-1 of rnd over sl st, ch 1.

Rnd 11 (Sl st, ch 4, dc) in first ch-1, *2-dc V in next ch-1, ch 1, 2-dc V in next ch-1, ch 3, sc in next ch-1, [ch 4, sc in next ch-1] 4 times, ch 3, 2-dc V in next ch-1, ch 1, 2-dc V in next ch-1, ch 1; rep from * end, 2-dc V in last ch-1, ch 1.

Rnd 12 (Sl st, ch 4, dc) in first ch -1, *[ch 1, 2-dc V in ch-1 of next 2-dc V] twice, ch 3, sc in next ch-4, [ch 4, sc in next ch-4] 3 times, ch 3, 2-dc V in ch-1 of next 2-dc V, ch 1, 2-dc V in ch-1 of next 2-dc V; rep from *, end 2-dc V in ch-1 of last 2-dc V, ch 1.

Rnd 13 (Sl st, ch 4, dc) in first ch-1, *ch 3, 2-dc V in ch-1 of next 2-dc V, ch 1, 2-dc V in ch-1 of next 2-dc V, ch 3, sc in next ch-4, [ch 4, sc in next ch-4] twice, ch 3, 2-dc V in ch-1 of next 2-dc V, ch 1, 2-dc V in ch-1 of next 2-dc V; rep from *, end 2-dc V in ch-1 of last 2-dc V, ch 1.

Rnd 14 (Sl st, ch 4, dc) in first ch-1, ch 6, 2-dc V in ch-1 of next 2-dc V, *ch 2, 2-dc V in next ch-1, ch 3, sc in next ch-4, ch 4, sc in next ch-4, ch 3, 2-dc V in ch-1 of next 2-dc V, ch 2, 2-dc V in ch-1 of next 2-dc V, ch 6, 2-dc V in ch-1 of next 2-dc V; rep from *, end 2-dc V in ch-1 of last 2-dc V, ch 2.

Rnd 15 (Sl st, ch 4, dc) in first ch-1, *ch 1, 7 dc in next ch-6, ch 1, 2-dc V in next ch-1, ch 3, 2-dc V in next ch-1, ch 3, sc in next ch-4, ch 3, 2-dc V in next ch-1, ch 3, 2-dc V in next ch-1; rep from *, end 2-dc V in last ch-1, ch 3.

Rnd 16 (Sl st, ch 4, dc) in first ch-1, *ch 2, dc in next dc, [ch 1, dc in next dc] 6 times, ch 2, 2-dc V in ch-1 of next 2-dc V, ch 3, [2-dc V in ch-1 of next 2-dc V] twice, ch 3, 2-dc V in ch-1 of next 2-dc V; rep from *, end 2-dc V in ch-1 of last 2-dc V, ch 3.

Rnd 17 (Sl st, ch 4, dc) in first ch-1, *ch 3, sc in next ch-1, [ch 4, sc in next ch-1] 5 times, ch 3, 2-dc V in next ch-1, ch 3, [2-dc V in next ch-1] twice; ch 3, 2-dc V in next ch-1, ch 3; rep from *, end 2-dc V in last ch-1, ch 3.

Rnd 18 (Sl st, ch 4, dc) in first ch-1, *ch 3, sc in next ch-4, [ch 4, sc in next ch-4] 4 times, ch 3, 2-dc V in next ch-1, ch 4, 2-dc V in next ch-1, ch 1, 2-dc V in next ch-1, ch 4, 2-dc V in next ch-1; rep from *, end 2-dc V in last ch-1, ch 4.

Rnd 19 (Sl st, ch 4, dc) in first ch-1, *ch 3, sc in next ch-4, [ch 4, sc in next ch-4] 3 times, ch 3, 2-dc V in next ch-1, ch 4, 2-dc V in next ch-1, ch 3, sk next ch-1, 2-dc V in next ch-1, ch 4, 2-dc V in next ch-1; rep from *, end 2-dc V in last ch-1, ch 4.

Rnd 20 (Sl st, ch 4, dc) in first ch-1, *ch 3, sc in next ch-4, [ch 4, sc in next ch-4] twice, ch 3, 2-dc V in next ch-1, ch 4, 2-dc V in next ch-1, ch 7, 2-dc V in next ch-1, ch 4, 2-dc V in next ch-1; rep from *, end 2-dc V in last ch-1, ch 4.

Rnd 21 (Sl st, ch 4, dc) in first ch-1, *ch 3, sc in next ch-4, ch 4, sc in next ch-4, ch 3, 2-dc V in next ch-1, ch 4, 2-dc V in next ch-1, ch 1, 8 dc in next ch-7, ch 1, 2-dc V in next ch-1, ch 4, 2-dc V in next ch-1; rep from *, end 2-dc V in last ch-1, ch 4.

Rnd 22 (Sl st, ch 4, dc) in first ch-1, *ch 3, sc in next ch-4, ch 3,

2-dc V in next ch-1, ch 5, 2-dc V in next ch-1, ch 2, dc in next dc, [ch 1, dc in next dc] 7 times, ch 2, 2-dc V in next ch-1, ch 5, 2-dc V in next ch-1; rep from *, end 2-dc V in last ch-1, ch 5.

Rnd 23 (Sl st, ch 4, dc) in first ch-1, *2-dc V in next ch-1, ch 5, 2-dc V in next ch-1, ch 3, sc in next ch-1, [ch 4, sc in next ch-1] 6 times, ch 3, 2-dc V in next ch-1, ch 5, 2-dc V in next ch-1; rep from *, end 2-dc V in last ch-1, ch 5.

Rnd 24 (Sl st, ch 4, dc) in first ch-1, *ch 1, 2-dc V in next ch-1, ch 5, 2-dc V in next ch-1, ch 3, sc in next ch-4, [ch 4, sc in next ch-4] 5 times, ch 3, 2-dc V in next ch-1, ch 5, 2-dc V in next ch-1; rep from *, end 2-dc V in last ch-1, ch 5.

Rnd 25 (Sl st, ch 4, dc) in first ch-1, *ch 2, 2-dc V in ch-1 of next 2-dc V, ch 5, 2-dc V in next ch-1, ch 3, sc in next ch-4, [ch 4, sc in next ch-4] 4 times, ch 3, 2-dc V in next ch-1, ch 5, 2-dc V in next ch-1; rep from *, end 2-dc V in last ch-1, ch 5.

Rnd 26 (Sl st, ch 4, dc) in first ch-1, *ch 4, 2-dc V in next ch-1, ch 5, 2-dc V in next ch-1, ch 3, sc in next ch-4, [ch 4, sc in next ch-4] 3 times, ch 3, 2-dc V in next ch-1, ch 5, 2-dc V in next ch-1; rep from *, end 2-dc V in last ch-1, ch 5.

Rnd 27 (Sl st, ch 4, dc) in first ch-1, *ch 8, 2-dc V in next ch-1, ch 6, 2-dc V in next ch-1, ch 3, sc in next ch-4, [ch 4, sc in next ch-4] twice, ch 3, 2-dc V in next ch-1, ch 6, 2-dc V in next ch-1; rep from *, end 2-dc V in last ch-1, ch 6.

Rnd 28 (Sl st, ch 4, dc) in first ch-1, *ch 1, 9 dc in ch-8, ch 1, 2-dc V in next ch-1, ch 6, 2-dc V in next ch-1, ch 3, sc in next ch-4, ch 4, sc in next ch-4, ch 3, 2-dc V in next ch-1, ch 6, 2-dc V in next ch-1; rep from *, end 2-dc V in last ch-1, ch 6.

Rnd 29 (Sl st, ch 4, dc) in first ch-1, *ch 2, dc in next dc, [ch 1, dc in next dc] 8 times, ch 2, 2-dc V in ch-1 of next 2-dc V, ch 6, 2-dc V in next ch-1, ch 3, sc in next ch-4, ch 3, 2-dc V in next ch-1, ch 6, 2-dc V in next ch-1; rep from *, end 2-dc V in last ch-1, ch 6.

Rnd 30 (Sl st, ch 4, dc) in first ch-1, *ch 3, sc in next ch-1, [ch 4, sc in next ch-1] 7 times, ch 3, 2-dc V in next ch-1, ch 6, 2-dc V in next ch-1, 2-dc V in next ch-1, ch 6, 2-dc V in next ch-1; rep from *, end 2-dc V in last ch-1, ch 6.

Rnd 31 (Sl st, ch 4, dc) in first ch-1, *ch 3, sc in next ch-4, [ch 4, sc in next ch-4] 6 times, ch 3, 2-dc V in next ch-1, ch 6, 2-dc V in next ch-1, ch 1, 2-dc V in next ch-1, ch 6, 2-dc V in next ch-1; rep from *, end 2-dc V in last ch-1, ch 6.

Rnd 32 (Sl st, ch 4, dc) in first ch-1, *ch 3, sc in next ch-4, [ch 4, sc in next ch-4] 5 times, ch 3, 2-dc V in next ch-1, ch 7, 2-dc V in next ch-1, ch 2, 2-dc V in ch-1 of next 2-dc V, ch 7, 2-dc V in next ch-1; rep from *, end 2-dc V in last ch-1, ch 7.

Rnd 33 (Sl st, ch 4, dc) in first ch-1, *ch 3, sc in next ch-4, [ch 4, sc in next ch-4] 4 times, ch 3, 2-dc V in next ch, ch 7, 2-dc V in next ch-1, ch 3, 2-dc V in next ch-1, ch 7, 2-dc V in next ch-1; rep from *, end 2-dc V in last ch-1, ch 7.

Rnd 34 (Sl st, ch 4, dc) in first ch-1, *ch 3, sc in next ch-4, [ch 4, sc in next ch-4] 3 times, ch 3, 2-dc V in next ch-1, ch 7, 2-dc V in next ch-1, ch 5, 2-dc V in next ch-1, ch 7, 2-dc V in next ch-1; rep from *, end 2-dc V in last ch-1, ch 7.

Rnd 35 (Sl st, ch 4, dc) in first ch-1, *ch 3, sc in next ch-4, [ch 4, sc in next ch-4] twice, ch 3, 2-dc V in next ch-1, ch 7, 2-dc V in next ch-1, ch 9, 2-dc V in next ch-1, ch 7, 2-dc V in next ch-1; rep from *, end 2-dc V in last ch-1, ch 7.

Rnd 36 (Sl st, ch 4, dc) in first ch-1, *ch 3, sc in next ch-4, ch 4, sc in next ch-4, ch 3, 2-dc V in next ch-1, ch 7, 2-dc V in next ch-1,

ch 1, 9 dc in next ch-9, ch 1, 2-dc V in next ch-1, ch 7, 2-dc V in next ch-1; rep from *, end 2-dc V in last ch-1, ch 7.

Rnd 37 (Sl st, ch 4, dc) in first ch-1, *ch 3, sc in next ch-4, ch 3, 2-dc V in next ch-1, ch 8, 2-dc V in next ch-1, ch 2, dc in next dc, [ch 1, dc in next dc] 8 times, ch 2, 2-dc V in ch-1 of next 2-dc V, ch 8, 2-dc V in next ch-1; rep from *, end 2-dc V in last ch-1, ch 8.

Rnd 38 (Sl st, ch 4, dc) in first ch-1, *2-dc V in next ch-1, ch 8, 2-dc V in next ch-1, ch 3, sc in next ch-1, [ch 4, sc in next ch-1] 7 times, ch 3, 2-dc V in next ch-1, ch 8, 2-dc V in next ch-1; rep from *, end 2-dc V in last ch-1, ch 8.

Rnd 39 (Sl st, ch 4, dc) in first ch-1, *ch 1, 2-dc V in next ch-1, ch 8, 2-dc V in next ch-1, ch 3, sc in next ch-4, [ch 4, sc in next ch-4] 6 times, ch 3, 2-dc V in next ch-1, ch 8, 2-dc V in next ch-1; rep from *, end 2-dc V in last ch-1, ch 8.

Rnd 40 (Sl st, ch 4, dc) in first ch-1, *ch 2, 2-dc V in ch-1 of next 2-dc V, ch 8, 2-dc V in next ch-1, ch 3, sc in next ch-4, [ch 4, sc in next ch-4] 5 times, ch 3, 2-dc V in next ch-1, ch 8, 2-dc V in next ch-1; rep from *, end 2-dc V in last ch-1, ch 8.

Rnd 41 (Sl st, ch 4, dc) in first ch-1, *ch 3, 2-dc V in next ch-1, ch 8, 2-dc V in next ch-1, ch 3, sc in next ch-4, [ch 4, sc in next ch-4]

4 times, ch 3, 2-dc V in next ch-1, ch 8, 2-dc V in next ch-1; rep from *, end 2-dc V in last ch-1, ch 8.

Rnd 42 (Sl st, ch 4, dc) in first ch-1, *ch 5, 2-dc V in next ch-1, ch 9, 2-dc V in next ch-1, ch 3, sc in next ch-4, [ch 4, sc in next ch-4] 3 times, ch 3, 2-dc V in next ch-1, ch 9, 2-dc V in next ch-1; rep from *, end 2-dc V in last ch-1, ch 9.

Rnd 43 (Sl st, ch 4, dc) in first ch-1, *ch 9, 2-dc V in next ch-1, ch 9, 2-dc V in next ch-1, ch 3, sc in next ch-4, [ch 4, sc in next ch-4] twice, ch 3, 2-dc V in next ch-1, ch 9, 2-dc V in next ch-1; rep from *, end 2-dc V in last ch-1, ch 9.

Rnd 44 (Sl st, ch 4, dc) in first ch-1, *ch 9, 2-dc V in next ch-1, ch 9, 2-dc V in next ch-1, ch 3, sc in next ch-4, ch 4, sc in next ch-4, ch 3, 2-dc V in next ch-1 sp, ch 9, 2-dc V in next ch-1; rep from *, end 2-dc V in last ch-1, ch 9.

Rnd 45 (Sl st, ch 4, dc) in first ch-1, *ch 9, 2-dc V in next ch-1, ch 9, 2-dc V in next ch-1, ch 3, sc in next ch-4, ch 3, 2-dc V in next ch-1, ch 9, 2-dc V in next ch-1; rep from *, end 2-dc V in last ch-1, ch 9.

Rnd 46 (Sl st, ch 4, dc) in first ch-1, *ch 9, 2-dc V in next ch-1; rep from *, end ch 9—64 (72) 2-dc V.

CHART 1

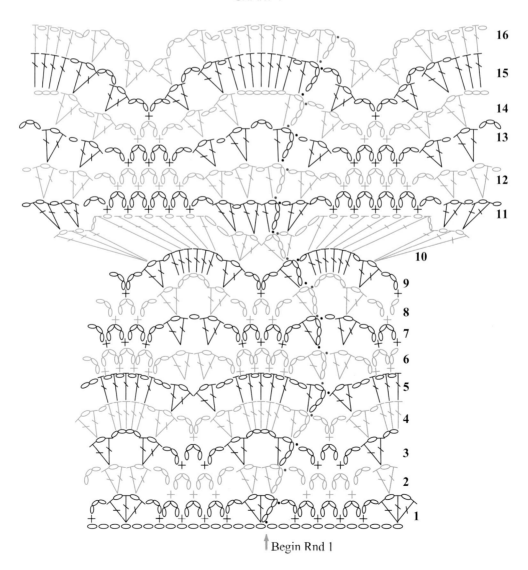

Begin Rnd 1

Rnd 47 (Sl st, ch 4, dc) in first ch-1, [ch 9, 2-dc V in next ch-1] 36 (40) times, [ch 9, dc in next ch-1, sl st in ch-1 directly opposite, dc in same ch-1 as dc] 7 (8) times, [ch 9, 2-dc V in next ch-1] 10 (12) times, [ch 9, dc in next ch-1, sl st in ch-1 directly opposite, dc in same ch-1 as dc] 7 (8) times, [ch 9, 2-dc V in next ch-1] twice, ch 9, join rnd with sl st in 3rd ch of beg ch-9. Fasten off.

FINISHING
Neck edge
Rnd 1 Work 192 (216) sc evenly spaced around neck edge. Join rnd with sl st in first sc.
Rnd 2 Sc in each of first 4 sc, picot (ch 3, sl st in first ch), *sc in each of next 4 sc, picot; rep from * around, join rnd with sl st in first sc. Fasten off.

Cuff trim
Work on each side.
Rnd 1 Join yarn with sl st in ch-1 sp nearest the fold, ch 1, sc in same ch-1, [5 sc in next ch-9, sc in next ch-1] 4 times, 3 sc in next ch-9, 3 sc in ch-9 directly opposite, working up back of cuff, [sc in next ch-1, 5 sc in next ch-9] 3 times, join rnd with sl st in first sc. Ch 3, turn—49 sc.

Rnd 2 Dc in each of next 26 sc, dc2tog, dc in each dc to end. Join rnd with sl st in top of beg-ch. Ch 1, turn—48 dc.
Rnd 3 Sc in same dc as join and in each dc around. Join rnd with sl st in first sc. Ch 3, turn—48 sc.
Rnd 4 Ch 3, dc in each sc around. Join rnd with sl st in top of beg-ch. Ch 1, turn.
Rnds 5 and 6 Rep rnds 2 and 3.
Rnd 7 Rep rnd 2 of neck edge.

Waistband
Rnd 1 Join yarn with sl st at side of lower opening where the 2 sides are joined, ch 1, sc in same sp, sc around entire bottom opening working 7 sc in each ch-9 and 1 sc in each ch-1. Join rnd with sl st in first sc—176 (208) sc.
Rnd 2 Ch 3, dc in each dc around. Join rnd with sl st in top of beg-ch.
Rnd 3 Ch 1, sc in same sc as join and in each dc around. Join rnd with sl st in first sc.
Rnds 4–8 (12) Rep rnds 2 and 3 for 2 (4) times, then rnd 2 once more.
Rnd 9 (13) Rep rnd 2 of neck edging.•

CHART 2

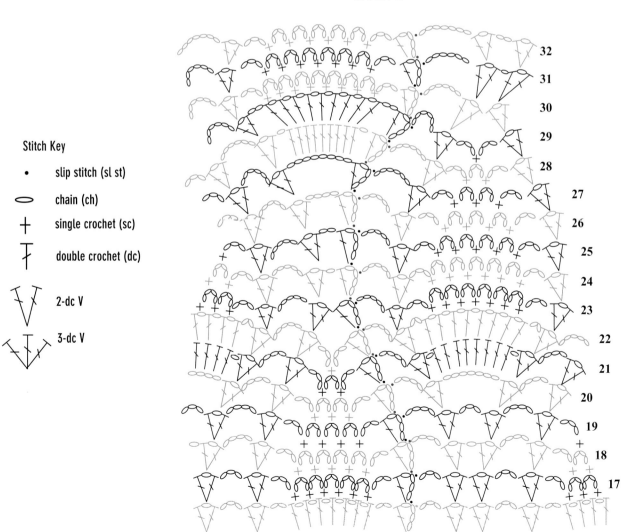

Stitch Key
- **•** slip stitch (sl st)
- ⬯ chain (ch)
- ✚ single crochet (sc)
- ✝ double crochet (dc)
- ⋎ 2-dc V
- ⋎ 3-dc V

CHART 3

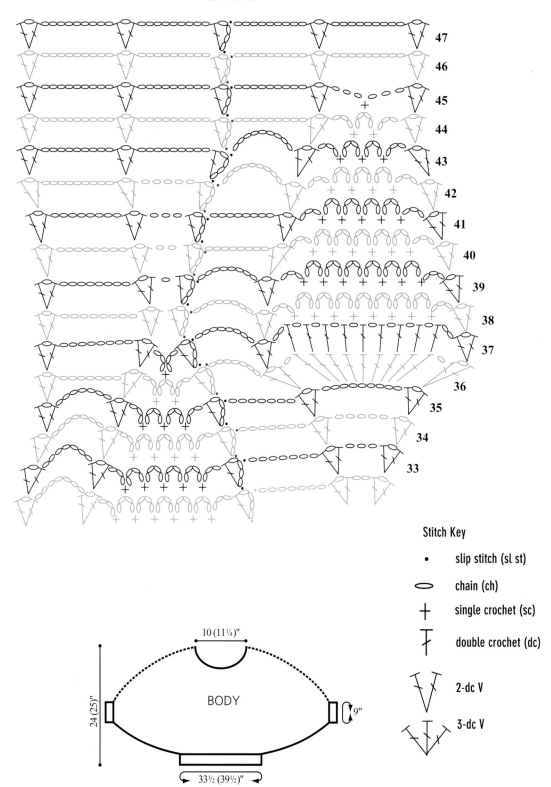

Stitch Key

- slip stitch (sl st)
⬭ chain (ch)
✝ single crochet (sc)
𝕋 double crochet (dc)
⋎ 2-dc V
⋎ 3-dc V

SLOUCHY HAT

Leaf stitch, worked into the rows below, melds the three-color stripe sequence of Lori Steinberg's slouchy hat. The crown is shaped with decreases and topped with a fluffy pom-pom.

●●●
INTERMEDIATE

SIZE
Instructions are written for one size.

FINISHED MEASUREMENTS
• Brim circumference 21"/53.5cm
• Length 10"/25.5cm

MATERIALS
• 2 1¾oz/50g hanks (each approx 87yd/80m) of Bergère de France *Magic Plus* (acrylic/combed wool) in #245-421 lichen (A-green), #254-611 criquet (B-brown), and #233-081 brebis (C-cream) 🔒
• Size I/9 (5.5mm) hook *OR SIZE TO OBTAIN GAUGE*
• Size G/6 (4mm) hook
• Stitch marker

GAUGE
13 sts and 14 rnds = 4"/10 cm over pat st using larger hook.
TAKE TIME TO CHECK GAUGE.

STITCH GLOSSARY
Back Post Single Crochet (BPsc) Insert hook from back to front to back around post of next st, yo, pull up lp, yo, draw through 2 lps.
Front Post Single Crochet (FPsc) Insert hook from front to back to front around post of next st, yo, pull up lp, yo, draw through 2 lps.
Make leaf Pick up 5 lps by inserting hook as foll: 2 sts to right of next st and 1 row down, 1 st to right and 2 rows down, directly below and 3 rows down, 1 st to left and 2 rows down, 2 sts to left and 1 row down, then insert hook in top of next st, yo and draw through lp, yo and draw through all 7 lps on hook.

PATTERN STITCH (multiple of 6 sts)
Rnds 1–3 With A, sc in each st around.
Rnd 4 With B, *sc in next 5 sts, make leaf; rep from * around.
Rnds 5–7 Rep rnds 1–3 with B.
Rnd 8 With C, sc in next 2 sts, *make leaf, sc in next 5 sc; rep from * to last 4 sts, make leaf, sc to end of rnd.

Rnds 9–12 Rep rnds 1–4 with C and A.
Rnds 13–16 Rep rnds 5–8 with A and B.
Rnds 17–20 Rep rnds 1–4 with B and C.
Rnds 21–24 Rep rnds 5–8 with C and A.
Rep rnds 1–24 for pat st.

HAT
With A and larger hook, ch 84. Join with sl st, being careful not to twist sts and place marker for beg of rnds.
Working into 1 side of ch, sc in each ch around.

Beg pat st
Work rnds 1–24 of pat st, piece measures approx 7"/18cm from beg.

Crown shaping
Next (dec) rnd With A, sc in next 3 sts, [sk next sc, sc in next 5 sc] 14 times, sc to end—70 sc.
Next rnd Sc in each sc around.
Next (dec) rnd [Sc in next 4 sts, sk next st] 14 times—56 sts.
Next rnd With B, sc in next 3 sc, *make leaf; sc in next 7 sc; rep from * to last 5 sts, make leaf, sc in next 4 sts.
Next 3 rnds Sc, dec 7 sts evenly around—35 sts.
Next rnd With C, sc 3, *make leaf, sc in next 4 sts; rep from * to last 2 sc, make leaf, sc in last sc.
Next 3 rnds Sc dec 7 sts evenly around—14 sc.
Fasten off, leaving long tail.

BAND
With smaller hook and A, work in opposite side of beg chain, sc in each st around.
Next rnd *FPsc, BPsc; rep from * to end.
Rep last rnd 4 times more. Fasten off.

FINISHING
With C, make a 4"/10cm pom-pom. Attach pom-pom to center of crown using tail.•

SHORT-SLEEVE TOP

Wide azure stripes elevate Yoko Hatta's V-neck lace top. The body is worked in the round from the top down; the bodice is worked up from the foundation chain.

●●●
INTERMEDIATE

SIZE
Sized for Small, Medium/Large, 1X, 2X and shown in size Medium/Large.

FINISHED MEASUREMENTS
- Bust 40 (48, 56, 62)"/102 (122, 142, 158)cm
- Length 22 (23, 25, 25)"/56 (60, 64, 64)cm

MATERIALS
- 5 (7, 8, 10) 1¾oz/50g hanks (each approx 137yd/125m) of Fibra Natura/Universal Yarn *Flax* (linen) in #14 white (A) (3)
- 2 (2, 3, 3) hanks in #10 turquoise (B)
- Sizes C/2 and D/3 (2.75 and 3.25mm) hooks
OR SIZE TO OBTAIN GAUGE

GAUGES
- 18 dc and 10 rows = 4"/10cm over st pat for upper half with larger hook.
- 2 pat reps and 10 rows = 4"/10cm over st pat for lower half with larger hook
TAKE TIME TO CHECK GAUGES.

NOTE
Ch-3 counts as 1 dc throughout. Ch-5 counts as 1 dc plus ch-2 sp throughout.

STITCH GLOSSARY
Picot in Stitch Pattern B—Upper Fronts and Backs Ch 3, sl st in top of last sc or dc made.
Picot in Edging Ch 3, sl st in 3rd ch from hook.

LOWER BACK
With larger hook and A, ch 121 (145, 169, 193).
Row 1 Sc in 2nd ch from hook, *ch 5, sk 3 ch, sc in next ch; rep from * to end—30 (36, 42, 48) ch-5 sps. Ch 5, turn.
Row 2 Sc in first ch-5 sp, 7 dc in next ch-5 sp, sc in next ch-5 sp, *ch 5, sc in next ch-5 sp, 7 dc in next ch-5 sp, sc in next ch-5 sp; rep from * to end, ch 2, dc in last sc. Ch 1, turn.
Row 3 Sc in first dc, *ch 5, sk 1 dc, sc in next dc, ch 5, sk 3 dc, sc in next dc, ch 5, sc in next ch-5 sp; rep from * to end. Ch 5, turn.

Sizes Small and Medium/Large only
Row 4 Rep row 2.

Sizes 1X and 2X only
Rep rows 3 and 4 three times. Fasten off.

LOWER FRONT
Work same as for back, do not fasten off after row 4 (4, 10, 10), ch 1, turn.

Join front and back
Row 1 Sc in first dc, [ch 5, sk 1 dc, sc in next dc, ch 5, sk 3 dc, sc in next dc,*ch 5, sc in next ch-5 sp, ch 5, sk 1 dc, sc in next dc, ch 5, sk 3 dc, sc in next dc]; rep from * to end of Front, ch 5, sc2tog over last ch-5 sp of Front and first dc of back, rep instructions from [to] once more, ch 5, sc in last ch-5 sp, turn. Front and back are now worked as one, in rnds as foll.
Rnd 2 Sc in first ch-5 sp, 7 dc in next ch-5 sp, sc in next ch-5 sp, *ch 5, sc in next ch-5 sp, 7 dc in next ch-5 sp, sc in next ch-5 sp; rep from * to end, ch 2, dc in last sc, join rnd with sl st in first ch-5 sp. Ch 1, turn.
Rnd 3 Sc in dc, ch 5, sk 1 dc, sc in next dc, ch 5, sk 3 dc, sc in next dc, *ch 5, sc in next ch-5 sp, ch 5, sk 1 dc, sc in next dc, ch 5, sk 3 dc, sc in next dc; rep from * to end, ch 2, dc in first sc. Ch 1, turn.
Rnd 4 Sc in ch-2 sp, 7 dc in next ch-5 sp, sc in next ch-5 sp, *ch 5, sc in next ch-5 sp, 7 dc in next ch-5 sp, sc in next ch-5 sp; rep from * to end, ch 2, dc in first sc. Ch 1, turn.
Rep rnds 3 and 4 for pat until piece measures 14½ (16, 17½, 17½)"/37 (40.5, 44.5, 44.5)cm from foundation ch, ending with a rnd 4. Fasten off.

Upper left front
With larger hook and B, working in opposite side of foundation ch, join yarn with sl st in base of first sc.
Row 1 *Ch 5, sc in next ch-3 sp, picot; rep from * 14 (17, 20, 23) times more, ch 2, dc in next sc. Ch 3, turn.
Row 2 Dc in ch-2 sp, *ch 1, 3 dc in next ch-5 sp; rep from * to end, ch 1, dc in sp created by t-ch, sc in 3rd ch of t-ch. Ch 3, turn.
Row 3 Work 2 dc in first ch-1 sp, picot, dc in same ch-1 sp, *ch 1, 2 dc in next ch-1 sp, picot, dc in same ch-1 sp; rep from * to end, dc in top of t-ch. Ch 1, turn.
Row 4 Sc in first dc, ch 5, *sc in next ch-1 sp, ch 5; rep from * to end, sc in last dc. Ch 5, turn.
Row 5 Sc in first ch-5 sp, picot, *ch 5, sc in next ch-5 sp, picot; rep from * to end, ch 2, dc in last sc. Ch 3, turn.
Rows 6–8 Rep rows 2–4, change to A before final ch 5, turn of row 8.
Rows 9 and 10 With A, rep row 5 then row 2. Change to B before final ch 3, turn of row 10.
Rows 11–18 With B, rep rows 3–5, then rows 2–5, then row 2 once more. Change to A before final ch 3, turn of row 18.

Rows 19 and 20 With A, rep rows 3 and 4. Fasten off.

Upper right front

With larger hook and B, working in opposite side of foundation ch join yarn with sl st in base of same sc as final dc of row 1 of upper left front.

Row 1 *Ch 5, sc in next ch-3 sp, picot; rep from * 14 (17, 20, 23) more times, ch 2, dc in last sc. Ch 3, turn. Works same as for upper left front, starting with row 2.

Upper left and right back

Work same as for upper left and right front through row 19 only. Fasten off after row 19.

FINISHING

Join shoulder seams.

Row 1 With A and smaller hook, with RS of upper right back facing, sc in first dc, ch 2, sc in first ch-5 sp of front, *ch 2, sc in next ch-1 sp of back, ch 2, sc in next ch-5 sp of front; rep from * to end, ch 2, sc in last dc. Fasten off.

Rep join on other shoulder seam, beg at the neck edge and working out.

Edging

Work around each armhole opening and around all of neck edge as foll:

Rnd 1 With smaller hook and A, join yarn with sc in side of any dc, *ch 1, picot, ch 1, sc in next dc; rep from * around, anchoring edging with sc at base of each armhole and at base of front and back neck edge divide, ch 1, picot, ch 1, join rnd with sl st in first sc.•

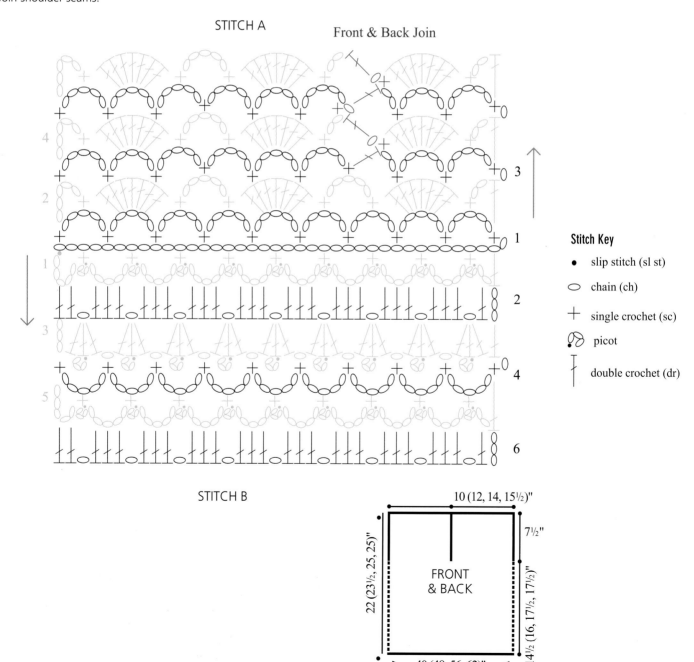

STITCH A

Front & Back Join

STITCH B

Stitch Key

- • slip stitch (sl st)
- ⌒ chain (ch)
- + single crochet (sc)
- ☌ picot
- ⊤ double crochet (dr)

10 (12, 14, 15½)"

7½"

22 (23½, 25, 25)"

FRONT & BACK

14½ (16, 17½, 17½)"

40 (48, 56, 62)"

MOTIF WRAP

Kathy Merrick's romantic medallion shawl is crocheted in a luxurious mohair and silk yarn. Because the motifs are joined to one another as they're completed, it's easy to customize the size of the shawl.

••
EASY

SIZE
Instructions are written for one size.

FINISHED MEASUREMENTS
Wrap is 20½ x 74"/52 x 188cm

MATERIALS
• 1 .88oz/25g ball (each approx. 229 yd/210m) of Rowan/Westminster Fibers *Kidsilk Haze* (super kid mohair/silk) each in #582 trance (A-blue), #651 forest green (B-dark green), #649 brick (C-pink), #644 ember (D-gold), #597 jelly (E-lime green), #596 marmalade (F-red-orange), #629 fern (G-medium green), and #581 meadow (H-pale green) ❶
• D/3 (3.25mm) hook *OR SIZE TO OBTAIN GAUGE*
• Rustproof pins

GAUGE
1 motif = 7¼"/18.5cm diameter using size D/3 (3.25mm) hook after blocking.
TAKE TIME TO CHECK GAUGE.

COLOR SEQUENCE
Change color at the end of rnds 2 and 3. See motif layout for color combinations.

STITCH GLOSSARY
Chain 7 Space Join (ch-7 sp join) Ch 3, sl st to adjoining motif's ch-7 sp, ch 3.
2 dc-cl (2 dc cluster) Yo and insert hook in next st, draw through a lp, yo and draw through 2 lps, yo and insert hook in same st, yo and draw through a lp, yo and draw through 2 lps (3 lps on hook) yo and draw through all 3 lps.
4 (5, 6) dc-cl (4 (5, 6) dc cluster) Yo and insert hook in next st, draw through a lp, yo and draw through 2 lps, [yo and insert hook in same st, yo and draw through a lp, yo and draw through 2 lps] 3 (4, 5) times more, yo and draw yarn through all lps on hook.
dtr (double treble) Yo hook 3 times, insert hook in st and draw through a lp (5 lps on hook); [yo and draw through 2 lps] 4 times.

MOTIF PATTERN (make 1, join 27)
Follow text below or chart.
Ch 8 with first color, sl st to first ch to form ring.
Rnd 1 (RS) Ch 3 (counts as dc), 23 dc in ring, sl st to top of t-ch, do not turn—24 dc.
Rnd 2 Ch 2, dc in top of t-ch, *ch 2, 2 dc-cl in next dc; rep from * around, ch 2, sl st to first dc, do not turn, fasten off first color—24 ch-2 sps.
Rnd 3 Join second color, ch 8 (counts as dtr, ch-3 sp), *dtr in 2 dc-cl, ch 3; rep from * around, sl st to 5th ch of t-ch, do not turn, fasten off second color—24 dtr.
Rnd 4 Join third color, ch 2, 4 dc-cl in same ch of t-ch, *ch 5, 5 dc-cl in next dtr; rep from * around, ch 2, dc in 4 dc-cl, do not turn—24 dc-cls.
Rnd 5 Ch 1, sc around post of dc, *ch 7, sc in next ch-5 sp; rep from * around ch 7, sl st to first sc, fasten off—24 ch-7 sps.

Joining motifs
Foll motif layout for location of adjoining motifs. Join 27 motifs by foll directions for a motif through rnd 4. In rnd 5, when next to an adjoining motif, substitute a ch-7 sp join for a ch-7 sp on the adjoining side of the motif (see joining diagram). This will seamlessly connect the two motifs. When connecting a motif to two different motifs, sk 1 ch-7 sp between previous join.

Edging

Join A to any ch-7 sp on a rnd 5 with a sl st. Ch 2, 5 dc-cl in same ch-7 sp, *[ch 9, 6 dc-cl in next ch-7 sp] around motif to joining, ch 9, sc in next ch-7 sp, ch 9, sc in next ch-7 sp on next motif; rep from * around wrap, sl st to top of dc-cl, fasten off.

Blocking

Immerse wrap in cold water. Place on towels and roll out excess water, do not wring. Pin wrap out to schematic size and allow to dry.•

Stitch Key

- •   slip stitch (sl st)
- ⬯   chain (ch)
- ✚   single crochet (sc)
- ⵜ   double crochet (dc)
- ⵟ   double treble crochet (dtr)

 2 double crochet cluster (2 dc-cl)

5 double crochet cluster (5 dc-cl)

6 double crochet cluster (6 dc-cl)

MOTIF DIAGRAM

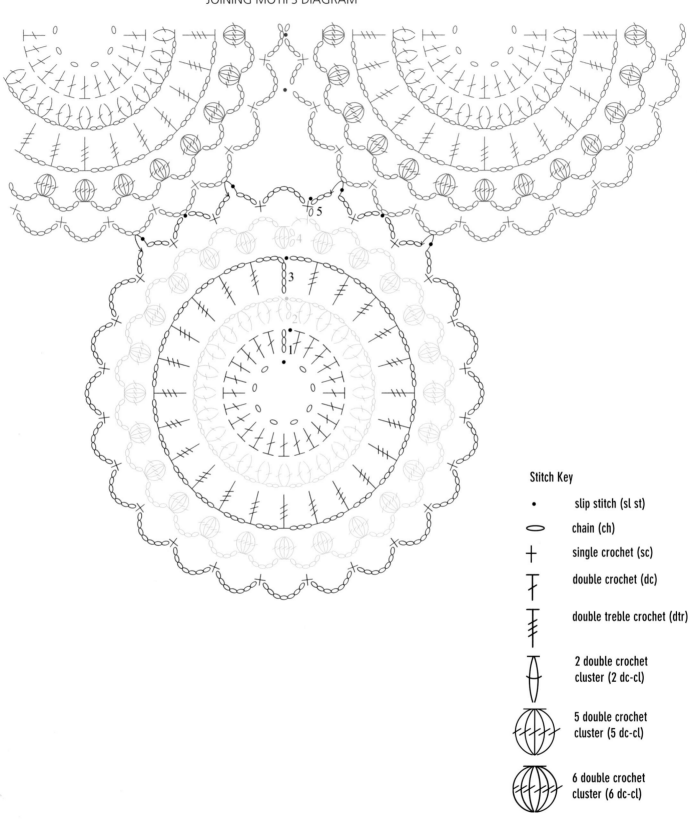

Stitch Key

•	slip stitch (sl st)
⬯	chain (ch)
+	single crochet (sc)
⊤	double crochet (dc)
‡	double treble crochet (dtr)
⟨⟩	2 double crochet cluster (2 dc-cl)
⬭	5 double crochet cluster (5 dc-cl)
⬭	6 double crochet cluster (6 dc-cl)

EDGING DIAGRAM

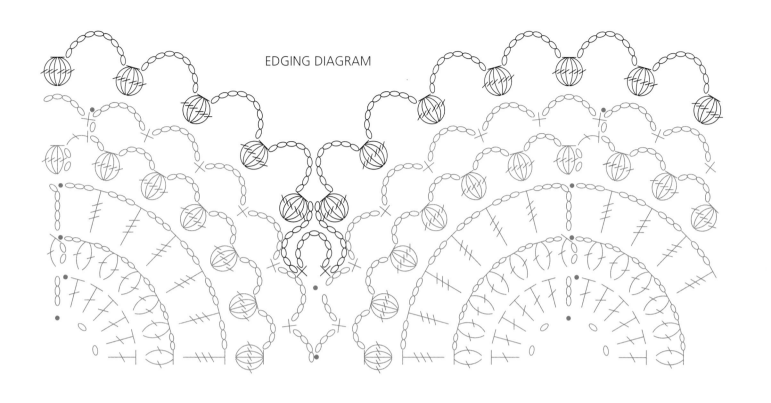

WRAP MOTIF LAYOUT

DGF	HBD	GFC	CBE	DHA	EFD	HCG	GHB	DAF
GBF	FHA	ECB	BAD	HEF	ACB	GAE	FEA	CDH	HGC
CDG	AEH	FBA	ADG	FGH	BDC	DHF	EBG	AED

ROSE BARRETTE

Yoko Hatta's delicate barrette features a central rose motif. She attached three of these blooms, nestled between a pair of leaves, to a crocheted casing that covers the back of a purchased metal barrette.

●●●
INTERMEDIATE

FINISHED MEASUREMENTS
• Length 4"/10cm

MATERIALS
• 1 2.8oz/80g ball (each approx 400yd/366m) of Aunt Lydia's *Crochet Thread Classic 10* (mercerized cotton) each in #419 ecru (A), #420 cream (B), and #424 peach (C) (⓪)
• Size 7 steel (1.5mm) crochet hook
• One size 7 (4.5mm) knitting needle for making flower centers
• 3"/7.5cm hair clip
• Sewing needle and thread

GAUGE
Gauge is not important for this project.

FLOWER MOTIF
Make 3 with rnds 1–4 in A, rnds 5 and 6 in B, rnd 7 in C.
Ch 6. Join ch with a sl st to 1st ch to form ring.
Rnd 1 (RS) Ch 1, work 12 sc in ring, join with sl st to ch 1.
Rnd 2 (RS) Ch 1, sc in next sc, *ch 3, sk 1 sc, sc in next sc; rep from * 4 times more, ch 3, join with sl st to ch 1.
Rnd 3 (RS) Ch 1, *(sc, hdc, 3 dc, hdc, sc) in ch-3 sp; rep from * 5 times more, join with sl st to ch 1, turn.
Rnd 4 (WS) BPsc around sc of rnd 2, *ch 5, BPsc around sc from rnd 2; rep from * 4 times, ch 5, join with sl to to BPsc, turn.
Rnd 5 (RS) Ch 1, *(sc, hdc, 5 dc, hdc, sc) in ch-5 sp; rep from * 5 times more, join with sl st to ch 1, turn.
Rnd 6 (WS) BPsc around BPsc of rnd 4, *ch 7, BPsc around BPsc from rnd 4; rep from * 4 times more, ch 7, join with sl st to BPsc, turn.
Rnd 7 (RS) Ch 1, *(sc, hdc, 7dc, hdc, sc) in ch-7 sp; rep from * 5 times more, join with sl st to ch 1. Fasten off.

FLOWER CENTER
Make 3 in A.
Wrap A around needle 8 times, remove from needle and work 16 sc into ring, join with a sl st to beg of rnd. Working over first rnd, work 14 sc into ring. Fasten off.

LEAF MOTIF
Make 2 in A.
Ch 15.
Row 1 Sc in 2nd ch from hook and in each of next 12 ch, 3 sc in last ch for leaf tip, cont along other side of ch, sc in each ch to 1 ch before end, turn—27 sc.
Row 2 Ch 1, sc in each sc to 1 st before tip, 3 sc in next sc, 1 sc in each sc to 2 scs before end, turn.
Rows 3–6 Rep row 2.
Fasten off.

CLIP CASING
With A, ch 10.
Row 1 Dc in 5th ch from hook and in next 5 chs, ch 3, turn.
Rows 2–7 Dc in next 5 dc, dc in top of t-ch, ch 3, turn.
Fasten off.

FINISHING
Using photo as guide, arrange Flower Motifs with Flower Centers on top of Leaf Motifs and sew together, allowing Leaf Motifs to extend on either side.
Sew clip casing around top bar of clip, then sew motifs to casing.●

MESH GAUNTLETS

Lori Steinberg begins her opera-length gauntlets at the bobbled cuff, continuing to the chain-mesh arms and ending with a double-crochet edging. Feed decorative leather stips, ribbons, or chains through eyelets at the edging bands.

●●●
INTERMEDIATE

FINISHED MEASUREMENTS
• Hand circumference 8½"/21.5cm
• Length 20"/51cm

MATERIALS
• 2 3½oz/100g hanks (each approx 197yd/180m) of Cascade Yarns *Eco Duo* (alpaca/wool) in #1704 chicory (🔲)
• G/6 (4mm) crochet hook *OR SIZE TO OBTAIN GAUGE*
• Stitch marker
• Four ⅛"/.3cm leather strips, each 18"/45.5cm long

GAUGE
15 sts and 8 rows = 4"/10cm over dc using size G/6 (4mm) hook. *TAKE TIME TO CHECK GAUGE.*

NOTES
Cuff and arm are worked in the round from the foundation chain, hand is worked in rows from the other side of the foundation chain and joined in the round when thumb opening is complete.

STITCH GLOSSARY
Petal group (pg) Work sc, hdc, 3 dc around post of next dc.

CUFF
Ch 28. Join with sl st and place marker (pm) for beg of rnd.
Rnd 1 Ch 3 (counts as dc), working in one side of ch only, dc in each ch around, join with sl st in beg ch 3.
Rnd 2 Work pg around post of next dc, sk 1 dc, *sl st in top of next dc, pg in same dc as sl st, sk 1 dc; rep from * around, join with sl st.
Rnd 3 Ch 3, dc in each dc around, join with sl st in beg ch 3.
Rep rnds 2 and 3 twice more, then rep rnd 1.

Beg mesh pat
Setup rnd *Ch 5, sk next 3 dc, sc in next dc; rep from * around.
Pat rnd *Ch 5, sc in next ch-sp; rep from * around.
Rep pat rnd until piece measures 18"/45.5cm from beg.

Upper arm band
Next rnd Ch 3, 4 dc in first ch-5 sp, then 5 dc in each ch-5 sp around, join with sl st in beg ch.

Next (eyelet) rnd Ch 3, dc in next dc, ch 1, sk 1 dc, *dc in next 4 dc, ch 1, sk 1 dc; rep from *, end dc in last 2 dc, join with sl st in beg ch.
Next rnd Ch 3, dc in each dc around. Fasten off.

HAND
Join yarn with sl st to unused edge of foundation ch, ch 3 (counts as dc), dc in each ch around, do not join—28 dc. Turn.
Next row Ch 3, dc in each dc across, turn.
Rep last row 3 times more. At end of last row, do not turn, ch 2 and join into rnd with sl st.
Next rnd Ch 3, dc in each dc around.
Next (eyelet) rnd Ch 3 (counts as dc), dc in next dc, *ch 1, sk 1 dc, dc in next 4 dc; rep from *, end dc in last 2 dc, join with sl st.
Next rnd Ch 3, dc in each dc around. Fasten off.

Thumb
Note Thumb is worked in rows from side to side of thumb opening and joined as you go.
Join yarn with sl st to beg of thumb opening, sl st around thumb opening as foll: 2 sts across bottom, 10 sts along side edge, 2 sts across top, 10 sts along opposite side edge.
Next row (RS) Ch 5, sk 2 bottom sl sts, join to sl st on opposite side. Sl st in next 3 sl sts along edge, turn.
Next row Ch 5, sc in ch-5 sp, ch 5, join to corresponding sl st on opposite side. Sl st in next 3 sts along edge, turn.
Next row Ch 5, [sc in next ch-5 sp, ch 5] twice, sl st in corresponding sl st, turn.
Next row Ch 3, [3 dc in ch-5 sp] 3 times, join to corresponding sl st, turn.
Next rnd (RS) Ch 1, sc in each dc across, then in each rem sl st along upper edge of thumb opening, join with sl st to ch 1. Fasten off.

FINISHING
Using photo as guide, thread leather strips through eyelet rnds at each end.●

LACE MEDALLION PILLOW COVERS

Vanessa Putt's circular lace medallions dress up store-bought
pillow covers in a variety of sizes—the circumference is easily altered by
working fewer or more mesh repeats before the final picot round.
The motifs are secured to the shams with matching sewing thread.

••
EASY

FINISHED MEASUREMENTS
• Square pillow 22 x 22"/56 x 56cm
• Rectangular pillow 12 x 20"/30.5 x 51cm

MATERIALS
• 1 2oz/55g hank (each approx 400yd/366m) of Jade Sapphire
Exotic Fibres *Mongolian Cashmere 2-ply* (cashmere) in #000 ivory
or #080 little boy blue (1 hank makes 4 medallions) (**1**)
• Size F/5 (3.75mm) crochet hook *OR SIZE TO OBTAIN GAUGE*
• 12 x 20"/30.5 x 51 pillow cover in blue or 22 x 22"/56 x 56cm
pillow cover in cream, pillow forms to fit covers
• Sewing needle and thread

GAUGE
1 medallion = 10½"/26.5cm after blocking.
TAKE TIME TO CHECK GAUGE.

STITCH GLOSSARY
Beg Tr Puff St (Beg TPS) *Yo twice, draw up a lp in same st, [yo
twice and draw through 2 lps] twice, leaving rem sts on hook; rep
from * 5 times more, yo and draw through all lps on hook.
Tr Puff St (TPS) *Yo twice, draw up a lp in same st, [yo twice and
draw through 2 lps] twice; rep from * 6 times more, yo and draw
through all lps on hook.
Dc Puff Cluster (DPC) [*Yo, draw up a lp in same st or sp, yo and
draw through 2 lps, leaving rem sts on hook; rep from * 4 times
more, yo and draw through all lps on hook].

MEDALLION
(make 2 in cream for rectangular pillow and 4 in blue for square
pillow)
Ch 3, join with sl st to first ch to form ring.
Rnd 1 Ch 3 (counts as first dc), work 11 dc into ring. Join with
sl st into top of beg ch.

Rnd 2 Ch 4, work Beg TPS in same st as sl st, *ch 5, sk next dc,
work TPS in next dc; rep from * 4 times more, end with ch 5, sl st
in top of Beg TPS—6 TPS and 6 ch-5 sps.
Rnd 3 Sl st in next ch-5 sp, ch 3 (counts as first dc), work 6 dc sts
in same ch-5 sp, *ch 3, work 7 dc sts in next ch-5 sp; rep from *
4 times more, end with ch 3, sl st in top of beg ch-3.
Rnd 4 Sl st in next 3 dc, ch 6, dc in same st, *ch 3, (DPC, ch 4,
DPC) in next ch-3 sp, ch 3, sk 3 dc, (dc, ch 3, dc) in next dc; rep
from * 4 times more, ch 3, (DPC, ch 4, DPC) in next ch-3 sp, ch 3,
sl st in 3rd ch of beg ch-6.
Rnd 5 Sl st in next ch-3 sp, ch 3 (counts as first dc), 4 dc in same
ch-3 sp, *ch 1, dc in next ch-3 sp, ch 1, 5 dc in next ch-4 sp, ch 1,
1 dc in next ch-3 sp, ch 1, 5 dc in next ch-3 sp; rep from * 4 times
more, ch 1, 1 dc in next ch-3 sp, ch 1, 5 dc in next ch-4 sp, ch 1,
1 dc in next ch-3 sp, ch 1, end with sl st in top of beg ch-3.
Rnd 6 Sl st in next 2 dc, ch 6, *dc in next ch-1 sp, ch 3, dc in next
ch-1 sp, ch 3, sk next 2 dc, dc in next dc, ch 3; rep from * around,
end dc in next ch sp, ch 3, dc in next ch-1 sp, ch 3, sl st in 3rd ch
of beg ch-6.
Rnd 7 Ch 7, *dc in next dc, ch 4; rep from * around, end with
sl st in 3rd ch of beg ch-7.
Rnd 8 Ch 3 (counts as first dc), 3 dc in next ch-4 sp, *sl st in next
dc, 4 dc in next ch-4 sp; rep from * around, end sl st at base and
sl st in top of beg ch-3.
Rnd 9 Ch 3, *DPC in next dc, ch 4, DPC in next dc, ch 3, sc in
next sl st, ch 3, sk next dc; rep from * around, end DPC in next dc,
ch 4, DPC in next dc,
sl st at base of beg ch-3. Fasten off.

FINISHING
Block motifs to measurements, pinning ch-4 sps of final row out
into points. With sewing needle and thread, using photo as guide,
tack medallions to covers (2 for rectangular pillow, 4 for square
pillow) connecting 3 points of each side where motifs touch.•

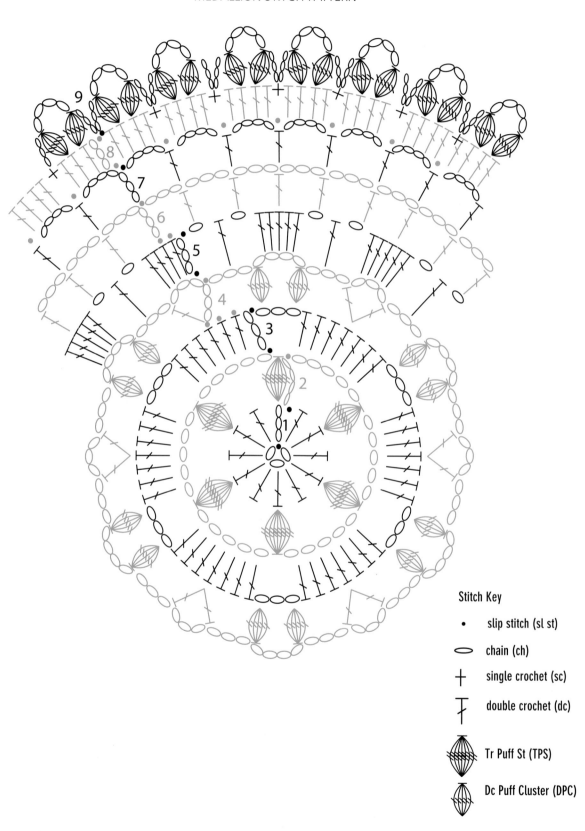

Stitch Key

- • slip stitch (sl st)
- ◯ chain (ch)
- ╂ single crochet (sc)
- ╤ double crochet (dc)

Tr Puff St (TPS)

Dc Puff Cluster (DPC)

WAVY RIPPLES PULLOVER

Dora Ohrenstein's lacy tunic carries a large ripple pattern that creates a striking visual effect. It works up quickly with double treble stitches. Make the neckline wider for an off-the-shoulder style.

●●●●
COMPLEX

SIZE
Sized for Small, Medium/Large, 1X, 2X and shown in size Small.

FINISHED MEASUREMENTS
- Bust 36 (42, 48, 54)"/91.5 (107, 122, 137)cm
- Length 25½ (25½, 29½, 29½)"/65 (65, 75, 75)cm
- Upper arm 16 (16, 20, 20)"/40.5 (40.5, 51, 51)cm

MATERIALS
- 8 (9, 12, 13) 1¾oz/50g hanks (each approx 200yd/183m) of Kollàge Yarns *Creamy* (milk/cotton) in #7140 natural (1)
- Size D/3 (3.25mm) hook *OR SIZE TO OBTAIN GAUGE*
- Safety pin or split ring stitch marker

GAUGE
19 sts/1 stitch repeat = 3"/7.5cm, 8 rows/1 row repeat = 4"/10cm using size D/3 (3.25mm) hook.
TAKE TIME TO CHECK GAUGE.

Gauge Swatch
Ch 41. Work rows 1–8 of body, without additional rep of starred instructions. Swatch will measure 6 x 4"/15 x 10cm.

NOTES
1) The rows of double treble stitches are slightly wider than other rows of this lace pattern, but the rows of single crochet stitches will draw in the overall width. This creates a waviness in the fabric.
2) Ch-6 counts as 1 dtr plus ch-1 throughout.

STITCH GLOSSARY
Special Sc (spsc) For first spsc in row, insert hook from back to front through both loops of sc, yo, draw up loop, complete sc as usual. Insert hook from front to back in same loops as sc just completed, then from back to front through both loops of next sc, yo, draw up loop, complete sc as usual. For last st in row, insert hook from front to back in same loops as sc just completed, then back to front in 3rd ch of t-ch.

BODY
Ch 231 (269, 307, 345).
Row 1 (RS) 4 dc in 4th ch from hook, *[dc in next ch, sk next ch] 8 times, dc in next ch, 5 dc in each of next 2 ch; rep from * 10 (12, 14, 16) times more, [dc in next ch, sk next ch] 8 times, dc in next ch, 5 dc in last ch—11 (13, 15, 17) ripples plus 2 half ripples. Ch 1, turn.

Row 2 Spsc in each dc across—228 (266, 304, 342) spsc. Ch 3, turn.
Row 3 4 dc in first sc, [dc in next sc, sk next sc] 8 times, dc in next sc, 5 dc in each of next 2 dc; rep from * 10 (12, 14, 16) times more, [dc in next sc, sk next sc] 8 times, dc in next sc, 5 dc in last sc. Ch 1, turn.
Row 4 Spsc in each dc across. Ch 6 (counts as 1 dtr plus ch-1 here and throughout), turn.
Row 5 [Dtr in first sc, ch 1] twice, dtr in same sc, *[sk 2 sc, dtr in next sc] 5 times, sk 2 sc, [dtr, ch 1] 3 times in next sc, dtr in same sc, [dtr, ch 1] 3 times in next sc, dtr in same sc; rep from * 10 (12, 14, 16) times more, [sk 2 sc, dtr in next sc] 5 times, sk 2 sc, [dtr, ch 1] 3 times in next sc, dtr in same sc. Ch 1, turn.
Row 6 Sc in each dtr and ch-1 sp across. Ch 6, turn.
Rows 7 and 8 Rep rows 5 and 6.
Row 9 Rep row 3.

Sizes Small and Medium/Large only
Rows 10–35 Rep rows 2–9 three times, then rows 2 and 3 once more. Ch 77 at end of row 35, remove hook and place lp on safety pin or split ring stitch marker.
Join new yarn with sl st at center of row 35 (in either dc at top of 6th (7th) ripple), ch 76. Fasten off.
Row 36 Place hook in lp on safety pin, turn. Sc in back or bump of 2nd ch from hook and in back or bump of each of next 75 ch, sc in first dc, spsc across body, sc in back or bump of each ch on opposite side. Ch 6, turn.
Rep rows 5–9 of pat then rows 2–9, then rows 2–4. Ch 1, turn at end of final row 4.

Sizes 1X and 2X only
Rows 10–39 Rep rows 2–9 three times, then rows 2–7 once more. Ch 96 (96) at end of row 39, remove hook, and place lp on safety pin or split ring stitch marker.
Join new yarn with sl st at center of row 39 (in either dtr at top of 8th (9th) ripple), ch 95 (95). Fasten off.
Row 40 Place hook in lp on safety pin, turn. Sc in back or bump of 2nd ch from hook and in back or bump of each of next 94 ch, sc in first dc, sc across body, sc in back or bump of each ch on opposite side—342 (361) sc. Ch 3, turn.
Rep row 9 of pat, then rows 2–9 twice, then rows 2–4. Ch 1, turn at end of final row 4.

All sizes
Last row Sc in first sc, *sc in next sc, sk next sc, sc in each of next

2 sc, sk next sc, hdc in each of next 2 sc, sk next sc, dc in each of next 2 sc, sk next sc, hdc in each of next 2 sc, sk next sc, [sc in each of next 2 sc, sk next sc] 3 times; rep from * across, working final instructions from [to] only twice, sk next sc, sc in last sc. Fasten off, leaving long tail for assembly. Back yoke and sleeves are completed.

FRONT YOKE AND SLEEVES

To set up, sew side seam of body with mattress st.

Row 1 With RS facing, work sc in opposite side of foundation ch of each st of back sleeve, spsc (spsc, sc, sc) across front body, then sc in opposite side of foundation ch of each st of opposite sleeve. Cont to end, foll instructions for your size, beg with row 37 (37, 41, 41).

FINISHING

Using long tails at end of each sleeve, stitch front sleeve to back sleeve beg at the cuff and stitching for 5 (5, 6, 6) ripples. Try the top on before completing seams, and adjust as needed for desired neck opening. Complete seams and sl st around neck opening.

Sleeve edging

Sizes Small and Medium/Large only

Attach yarn with sl st at foundation ch of sleeve, ch 1, sc in same place, *[(sc, ch 3) twice in side of next dtr row, (sc, ch 3) in next sc row)] twice, [(sc, ch 3) in next dc row, (sc, ch 3) in next sc row] twice, rep from * to seam at top of sleeve; sc in seam, [(sc, ch 3) in next sc row] twice, (sc, ch 3) in next dc, (sc, ch 3) in next sc row, rep again from * to beg of rnd, sl st to first sc in rnd. Fasten off.

Sizes 1X and 2X only

Attach yarn with sl st at foundation ch of sleeve, ch 1, sc in same place, [(sc, ch 3) in next dc row, (sc, ch 3) in next sc row] twice, *[(sc, ch 3) twice in next dtr row, (sc, ch 3) in next sc row)] twice, [(sc, ch 3) in next dc row, (sc, ch 3) in next sc row] twice, rep from * to seam at top of sleeve; sc in seam, [(sc, ch 3) in next sc row] twice, (sc, ch 3) in next dc, (sc, ch 3) in next sc row; rep again from * to beg of rnd, sl st to first sc in rnd. Fasten off.

Steam lightly to flatten seams, especially along top of sleeve. •

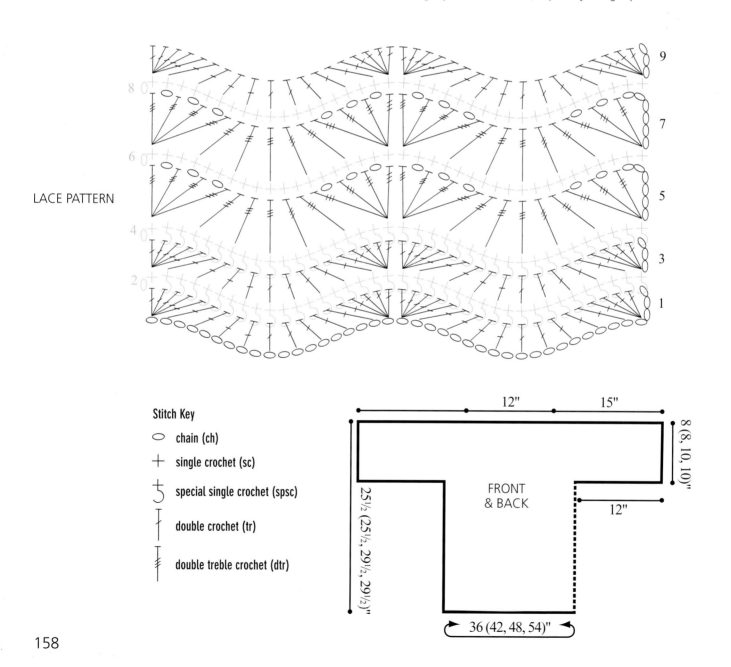

LACE PATTERN

Stitch Key

◯ chain (ch)

+ single crochet (sc)

⌐ special single crochet (spsc)

† double crochet (tr)

‡ double treble crochet (dtr)

12"   15"

FRONT & BACK

25½ (25½, 29½, 29½)"

8 (8, 10, 10)"

12"

36 (42, 48, 54)"

FILIGREE BRACELETS

Liven up your look by stitching a set of Pat Olski's Cruciani-style bracelets. With their minute put-up and eye-popping shades, mini skeins are the perfect fit for this project.

•
BEGINNER

SIZE
Instructions are written for one size.

FINISHED MEASUREMENTS
Approx 6½"/17cm long

MATERIALS
• One 10yd/9m skeinette (for each bracelet) of Koigu Wool Designs *KPM* (wool) each in #1000 royal blue, #1140 red, #1150 hot pink, #1155 pink, #1400 deep violet, #1521 lime, #1535 green, #2100 yellow, #2130 teal, #2220 orange **(1)**
• Crochet hook size D/3 (3.25mm) *OR SIZE TO OBTAIN GAUGE*

GAUGE
1 completed flower and 4-ch = ¾"/2cm.
TAKE TIME TO CHECK GAUGE.

BRACELET
Chain 6, join with sl st to first ch to form ring. Work 10 sc into ring, join sl st to last sc (loop closure).
Row 1 Ch 9, work sc in 5th ch from hook to form ring, ch 1 turn, sc in ring just made, [ch 5, sc in same ring] 3 times.
Row 2 Ch 9, work sc in 5th ch from hook to form ring, ch 1 turn, sc in ring just made, [ch 5, sc in same ring] twice. Rep rows 1 and 2 twice more, then row 1 once more.

Knotted end
Ch 10, in 2nd ch from hook work [yo, pull up a lp] 5 times, yo and draw through all lps on hook, pull tightly. Ch 1.
Turn work and work 1 sl st in each ch 8. Work along other side of bracelet as foll:
Row 1 Sc in the next ring, [ch 5, sc in same ring] twice, sl st in next 4 ch.
Row 2 Sc in the next ring, [ch 5, sc in same ring] 3 times, sl st in next 4 ch.
Rep rows 1 and 2 twice, then row 1 once.
Work 4 sl sts in next 4 ch, then sl st 1 into sc of ring. Fasten off.•

GRANNY SQUARE DRESS

Lean and clean are the watchwords for Mari Lynn Patrick's columnar dress. Side shaping is built into the whipstitched granny squares that sit between the armhole and waist; the plunging neckline can be sewn together for a less revealing look.

●●●●
COMPLEX

SIZE
Sized for Small, Medium, Large and shown in size Small.

FINISHED MEASUREMENTS
• Bust 34 (37, 39½)"/86 (94, 100)cm
• Hip 42½"/106.5cm
• Length 32½"/82.5cm

MATERIALS
• 4 (4, 5) 1¾oz/50g hanks (each approx 146yd/133m) of Blue Sky Fibers *Alpaca Silk* (alpaca/silk) each in #138 garnet (A) and #143 papaya (B) (3)
• 2 hanks each in #145 guava (C) and #144 mango (D)
• 1 hank each in #146 passion fruit (E) and #126 brick (F)
• One each size E/4 (3.5mm) and F/5 (3.75mm) hook
OR SIZES TO OBTAIN GAUGE

GAUGES
• 7 (3-dc) groups and 12 rows = 4"/10cm over granny pat st using larger hook.
• One 8-round basic square = 4¼"/10.75cm.
TAKE TIME TO CHECK GAUGES.

NOTE ON CONSTRUCTION
Squares are worked in two alternating colorways and joined by whipstitching the squares tog from the RS as each consecutive square is completed. See diagram for layout.

BASIC GRANNY SQUARE
Make a total of 50 basic squares, foll text below or chart, with 24 in color 1 and 26 in color 2. The color 1 squares are represented by the first set of letters. The (color 2) squares are represented by the letters in the parentheses.
With larger hook and E (F), ch 4, join with sl st in first ch to form ring.
Rnd 1 With E (F), [work 1 sc in ring, ch 3] 4 times, join with sl st to first sc.
Rnd 2 With E (F), sl st into the next ch-3 space, ch 3 (counts as 1 dc), 2 dc, ch 3 and 3 dc in same space for a corner, *(3 dc, ch 3, 3 dc) in next ch-3 space; rep from * twice more, join with sl st to top of beg ch-3. Cut E (F).
Rnd 3 With C (D), form a lp on hook, work sl st in corner space, then (1 sc, ch 3, 1 sc) in same corner space, *ch 3, 1 sc in between next 3rd and 4th dc's, ch 3, (1 sc, ch 3, 1 sc) in corner space; rep from *, ending ch 3, join with sl st to first sc.
Rnd 4 With C (D), sl st into corner space, ch 3 (counts as 1 dc),

2 dc, ch 3, and 3 dc in same space for corner, *3 dc in each ch-3 space to next corner, (3 dc, ch 3, 3 dc) in corner space; rep from *, end 3 dc in last space, join to top of beg ch-3. Cut C (D).
Rnd 5 With B, form a lp on hook, work sl st in corner space, then (1 sc, ch 3, 1 sc) in same corner space, *ch 3 and 1 sc in between next 3rd and 4th dc's to the next corner, (1 sc, ch 3, 1 sc) in corner space; rep from *, end ch 3, join with sl st to first sc.
Rnd 6 With B, rep rnd 4. Cut B.
Rnd 7 With A, rep rnd 5.
Rnd 8 With A, sl st into corner space, *work (1 sc, ch 3, 1 sc) in corner space, work 3 sc in each ch-3 space to corner; rep from * 3 times more, join with sl st to first sc. Do not cut A. Then after making the next square, from the RS use the end in A to whipstitch tog the adjoining squares (see diagram) by stitching through the inside lps only.

Decrease square
Make 6 total, 4 in color 1 and 2 in color 2. See diagram for placement of these decrease squares. The top part, or decreased part of the square, forms the decrease shaping along the waist and upper front edges.
Rnds 1–5 Work as for basic square.
Rnd 6 Work as for rnd 6 up to the 2nd corner, then in the 2nd corner work (3 dc, ch 3, 2 dc), then [2 dc in next ch-3 space] 4 times, in next corner work (2 dc, ch 3, 3 dc), then work 3 dc in each ch-3 space to end.
Rnd 7 Work as for rnd 7 up to the 2nd corner, then in the 2nd corner work (sc, ch 3, sc), [ch 2, sc between 2-dc groups] 5 times, ch 2, complete square as for basic square rnd 7.
Rnd 8 Work as for rnd 8 basic square only work 2 sc in each of the (6) ch-2 spaces.

PRE-FINISHING
After joining all the squares that make up the back, cont to work the shoulders and neck in granny pat st as foll:

UPPER BACK
Row 1 (RS) With larger hook, join C at the corner of the right upper back square 2, sc in same st with joining, ch 4, *sk 2 sts on square, sc in next st, ch 3; rep from * until there are 22 ch-lps, sc in last st, turn.
Row 2 (WS) With C, ch 3, 3 dc in each ch-3 space, end 1 dc in top of first sc, turn.
Row 3 With A, ch 1, *sc in first st, ch 3, 1 sc in between the next 2 (3-dc) groups; rep from *, end ch 3, sc in top of ch-3, turn.
Row 4 With A, rep row 2.

Note Rows 3 and 4 form the granny pat st which will be used as a 2-row pat on other edges of the dress.

Separate for neck
Right shoulder
Row 1 (RS) With E, work row 3 until there are 7 lps, turn.
Row 2 With E, rep row 2.
Row 3 With A, work row 3 until there are 6 lps, turn.
Row 4 With A, rep row 2.
Row 5 With D, work row 3 until there are 5 lps, turn.
Row 6 With D, rep row 2.
Rows 7 and 8 Work even on 5 (3-dc) groups with A.
Rows 9 and 10 Work even on 5 (3-dc) groups with B. Fasten off.

Left shoulder
Skip the center 8 (3-dc) groups, join E, and work 7 lps to end. Complete left shoulder as for right shoulder, shaping neck in reverse. From the WS, sl st the back shoulders to the front shoulders. Then, sew the side seams of front and back tog (using the whipstitch method as before).

Center front triangle
With larger hook and A, join to center square 2 from the RS and work 3 sc, 3 hdc, 4 dc, 1 tr, 4 dc, 3 hdc, 3 sc. These 22 sts form the triangle, the base for the neck trim.

SIDE FILLER
The side fillers are worked in the granny pat st as before, working in color stripes of *2 rows B, 2 rows A, 2 rows C, 2 rows A, 2 rows E, 2 rows A, 2 rows D, 2 rows A; rep from * (16 rows) for stripe pat as foll:
Row 1 With larger hook and B, join in top of first dec square and work a total of 12 (ch-3) lps.
Rows 2–5 Work in granny pat stripe st.
Dec row 6 Ch 3, 2 dc in first ch-3 space, [work 3 dc in each of next 2 spaces, 2 dc in next space] 3 times, 3 dc in each of last 2 spaces.
Row 7 Work even on 11 (ch-3) spaces.
Rows 8 and 9 Work even in granny pat stripe st.
Dec row 10 Work as for dec row 6 with 2 dc in 3 of the spaces evenly spaced.
Row 11 Work even on 10 (ch-3) spaces.

For size Large only
Rows 12–28 Work even on the 10 pats, fasten off. This completes the side filler for size Large.

For sizes Small and Medium only
Rows 12–14 Work even.
Dec row 15 Work as for dec row 6 with 2 dc in 3 of the spaces, evenly spaced.
Rows 16–18 Work even on 9 (ch-3) spaces.
Row 19 Work as for dec row 6 with 2 dc in 3 of the spaces, evenly spaced.
Rows 20–22 Work even on 8 (ch-3) spaces.

For size Medium only
Rows 23–28 Work even on the 8 pats. Fasten off. These complete the side filler for size Medium.

For size Small only
Row 23 Work as for dec row 6 with 2 dc in 3 of the spaces, evenly spaced.
Rows 24–26 Work even on the 7 pats.
Row 27 Work as for dec row 6 with 2 dc in 3 of the spaces, evenly spaced.
Row 28 Work even on 6 pats. Fasten off. This completes the side filler for size Small. Work other side filler in same way. Join the side fillers into the square of front and back by sc seam tog on the WS.

Armhole trim
With smaller hook and D, join to the underarm center of the armhole and work 29 (ch-3) lps around armhole. Join.
Rnd 2 With D, ch 3, work 3 dc in each ch-3 space.
Rnd 3 With C, ch 1, sc in first st, *ch 3, sk 2 sts, sc in next st, rep from * around.
Rnd 4 With A, work 3 sc in each ch-3 lp with an sc3tog in each (sc, ch 3, sc) at each corner space at the "square" corner of the armhole. Fasten off.

Neck trim
Row 1 With larger hook and D, work 51 (ch-3) lps around entire neck edge.
Row 2 With D, work 51 (3-dc) groups.
Rows 3 and 4 With A, work even in granny pat st.
Rows 5 and 6 With C, work even in granny pat st.
Rows 7 and 8 With A, work even in granny pat st. Fasten off, leaving long end of A. Sew the side edges of the neck trim to the center front triangle. Using the A yarn, seam the center front, closing up the V-opening as desired.•

GRANNY SQUARE STITCH PATTERN

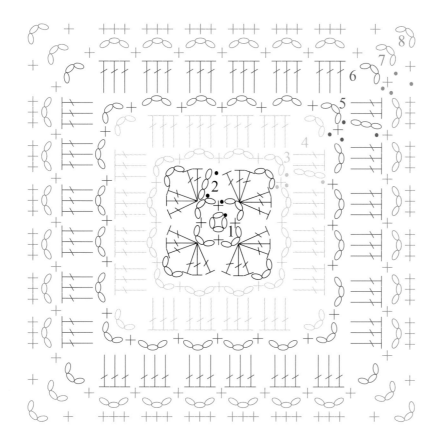

Stitch Key

- • slip stitch (sl st)
- ⬭ chain (ch)
- ┼ single crochet (sc)
- ⊤ double crochet (dc)

- • color E (F)
- • color C (D)
- • color B
- • color A

ASSEMBLY DIAGRAM

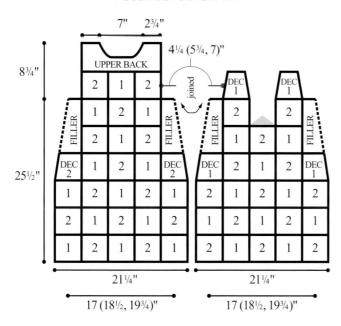

DIAGRAM KEY

1	Basic Granny Square in color 1
2	Basic Granny Square in color 2
DEC 1	Decrease Square in color 1
DEC 2	Decrease Square in color 2
▲	Center front triangle

BOBBLE CLUTCHES

Melody Ossola's retro-chic clutches, crocheted in a trio of colorways, are worked from the bottom up in bobbled rows separated by single crochet. A hand-sewn lining lends shape and strength.

FINISHED MEASUREMENTS
• Width at lower edge approx 8"/20cm
• Length without handles approx 5½"/12.5cm

MATERIALS
• 1 1¾oz/50g hank (each approx 175yd/160m) of Koigu Wool Designs *KPPPM* (wool) in #412 medium blues, #821 navy and aqua, OR #741 aqua and green ①
• Size H/8 (5mm) hook *OR SIZE TO OBTAIN GAUGE*
• Inazuma coin purse frames, size medium #1275 in #0 ivory, #15 jade, OR #1075 amber
• Small piece of fabric, sewing needle, and thread for lining

GAUGE
9 sts and 16 rows = 4"/10cm over bobble pat using size H/8 (5mm) hook.
TAKE TIME TO CHECK GAUGE.

BOBBLE STITCH
[Yo, insert hook in st, yo and draw up a lp, yo and draw through first 2 lps on hook] 4 times all in the same st, yo and draw through all 5 lps.

FIRST HALF
Ch 33. Work in bobble st as foll:
Row 1 (RS) Sc in 2nd ch from hook and in each ch to end—32 sc. Ch 1, turn.
Row 2 *Work bobble st in first st, sc in next st; rep from * across—16 bobble sts. Ch 1, turn.
Rows 3 and 5 Work sc in each st—32 sc. Ch 1, turn.

Row 4 *Sc in first st, bobble st in next st; rep from * across— 16 bobbles. Ch 1, turn. Rep rows 2–5 once more.
Dec row 10 (WS) Sc2tog, *work bobble st in next st, sc in next st; rep from * across to last 2 sts, sc2tog—14 bobble sts. Ch 1, turn.
Row 11 Sc in each st—30 sc. Ch 1, turn.
Rows 12–21 Rep rows 9 and 10 five times more, dec 1 st each side of every WS row—9 bobble sts.
Row 22 Sc in next st, sc2tog, sc in next 6 sts, sc2tog, sc in next 6 sts, sc2tog, sc in last st—17 sc. Fasten off.

SECOND HALF
With RS facing, join yarn and work sc along foundation ch—32 sc. Beg with row 4, work through row 22 as on first half. Fasten off.

FINISHING
Lay bag out flat and cut fabric to fit dimensions of bag, allowing for seams at side edges only. Fold lining in half with right sides tog and sew side seams approx 3¼"/8cm from fold. Fold bag in half with wrong sides tog, insert lining, and attach purse frame to top edges of bag, taking care to tuck in lining fabric with crocheted edge.

Join side edges of bag with sc as foll:
Joining row Working through both thicknesses, work sc directly into matching sts at the side edge, making sure to space them evenly and at the same depth so that all single crochet stitches are the same size—10 sc.
Bobble row *Work bobble in next st, sc in next st; rep from * up the sides of the bag, ending right under the purse frame joint—5 bobbles. Rep joining and bobble row on opposite edge of purse.•

PICOT-EDGED TANK AND BEADED NECKLACE

TANK

Yoko Hatta's amazing picot-edged tank is constructed from three different-sized squares turned 45 degrees to form a diamond grid.

●●●●
COMPLEX

SIZE
Sized for Small, Medium, Large and shown in size Small.

FINISHED MEASUREMENTS
• Bust 36 (40, 44)"/91 (102, 112)cm
• Length from underarm to lowest point 12 (13¾, 14¼)"/31 (35, 36)cm

MATERIALS
• 5 (7, 8) 1¾oz/50g balls (each approx 153yd/140m) of Rowan/Westminster Fibers *Siena 4-Ply* (cotton) in #651 white
• For size Small, sizes B/1 (2.25 mm), C/2 (2.75mm), and D/3 (3.25mm) hooks *OR SIZE TO OBTAIN GAUGE*
• For size Medium, sizes C/2 (2.75mm), D/3 (3.25mm), and E/4 (3.5mm) hooks *OR SIZE TO OBTAIN GAUGE*
• For size Large, sizes D/3 (3.25mm), E/4 (3.5mm), and F/5 (3.75mm) hooks *OR SIZE TO OBTAIN GAUGE*

GAUGES
• With size B/1 (2.25 mm) hook motif = 4.5"/11.5cm measured point to point.
• With size C/2 (2.75mm) hook motif = 5"/12.5cm measured point to point.
• With size D/3 (3.25mm) hook motif = 5½"/14cm measured point to point.
• With size E/4 (3.5mm) hook motif = 5¾"/14.5cm measured point to point.
• With size F/5 (3.75mm) hook motif = 6"/15.5cm measured point to point.
TAKE TIME TO CHECK GAUGES.

NOTE
Sizing is achieved by changing hook sizes. Choose the hook sizes you need for the size you wish to make and follow the assembly diagram.

STITCH GLOSSARY
Picot Ch 3, sl st in 3rd ch from hook.
2-dc cl (2-dc cluster) Yo and insert hook in next st, draw through a lp, yo and draw through 2 lps, yo and insert hook in same st, yo and draw through a lp, yo and draw through 2 lps (3 lps on hook) yo and draw through all 3 lps.

Stand-alone motif
Foll chart or text below.
With specified hook size, ch 5, join into ring with sl st in first ch.
Rnd 1 Ch 5, [dc in ring, ch 2] 7 times, join rnd with sl st in 3rd ch of beg-ch—8 ch-2 sps.
Rnd 2 Ch 3, 2 dc in same ch-sp as sl st, ch 2, (2-dc cl, ch 3, 2-dc cl) in next dc, *ch 2, 3 dc in next dc, ch 2, (2-dc cl, ch 3, 2-dc cl) in next dc; rep from * twice more, ch 2, join rnd with sl st in top of beg-ch.
Rnd 3 Ch 3, dc in same ch-sp as sl st, dc in next dc, 2 dc in next dc, ch 3, sk ch-2 sp, (2-dc cl, ch 3, 2-dc cl) in next ch-3 sp, *ch 3, sk ch-2 sp, 2 dc in next dc, dc in next dc, 2 dc in next dc, ch 3, sk ch-2 sp, (2-dc cl, ch 3, 2-dc cl) in next ch-3 sp; rep from * twice more, ch 1, join rnd with hdc st in top of beg-ch.
Rnd 4 Ch 1, sc in side of hdc at end of rnd 3, *ch 5, sk 2 dc, sc in next dc, ch 5, sc in next ch-3 sp, ch 5, (2-dc cl, ch 3, 2-dc cl) in next ch-3 sp, ch 5, sc in next ch-3 sp; rep from * 3 times more, ch 2, dc in first sc of rnd.
Rnd 5 +Ch 1, sc in top of last dc of rnd 4, [ch 5, sc in next ch-5 sp] 3 times, ch 5, sc in next ch-3 sp+, ch 5, sc in same ch-3 sp, *[ch 5, sc in next ch-5 sp] 4 times, ch 5, sc in next ch-3 sp, ch 5, sc in same ch-3 sp; rep from * twice more, ch 5, sl st in first sc of rnd. Fasten off.

Join-as-you-go motif
Work rnds 1–4 of stand-alone motif.
Line up motif in progress with motif to which you need to attach.
Rnd 5 Rep instructions from + to + in rnd 5 of stand-alone motif, *sc in adjacent corner ch-5 sp, ch 2, sc in same ch-5 sp on working motif, [ch 2, sc in adjacent ch-5 sp on opposite motif, ch 2, sc in next ch-5 sp on working motif] 5 times, ch 2, sc in adjacent corner ch-5 sp, ch 2, sc in same ch-5 sp on working motif; rep from * if an additional side needs to be joined, or if no joining is needed, cont around as for stand-alone motif.
Cont in this way, joining the working motif to an adjacent motif if needed, or working as for the stand-alone motif if no join is necessary.

TANK TOP

Select crochet hooks needed for your size. Work 44 motifs as shown on the diagram, using the smallest hook for your size for motifs marked A, the medium hook for your size for motifs marked B, and the largest hook for your size for motifs marked C.

FINISHING

Upper edging

With RS facing, and smallest hook, attach yarn in any open ch-5 sp in underarm area, left of the V shaping.

Rnd 1 Work 1 rnd sc evenly spaced around entire upper edge of tank by working 4 sc in each open ch-5 sp, 2 sc in each ch-5 sp where motifs are joined, and 5 sc in each of the 4 top points where the straps will be sewn; 2 points on front and 2 points on back. Join rnd with sl st in first sc. Ch 1, do not turn.

Rnd 2 Sc in each of next 2 sc, ch 1, picot, ch 1, *[sk 2 sc, sc in each of next 2 sc, ch 1, picot, ch 1]; rep from [to] until point is reached, sk 2 sc (last sc of 4 sc in ch-5 p before point plus first of 5 sc in point), sc in each of next 2 sc, ch 1, picot, ch 1, sc in next sc, ch 1, picot, ch 1, rep from [to] until bottom of V is reached, sk 2 sc, sc2tog; rep from * to end, join rnd with sl st in first sc. Fasten off.

Lower edging

With RS facing and smallest hook, attach yarn in any open ch-5 sp to the left of the V shaping.

Rnd 1 Ch 1, 2 sc in same ch-5 sp, ch 2, picot, ch 2, [2 sc in next ch-5 sp, ch 2, picot, ch 2]; rep from [ ] until point is reached, 2 sc in next ch-5 sp (point), ch 2, picot, ch 2, 2 sc in same ch-5 sp, ch 2, picot, ch 2, rep from [ ] until V is reached, sc in first of 2 joined ch-5 sps, ch 2, picot, ch 2, sc in 2nd of 2 joined ch-5 sps, ch 2, picot, ch 2; rep from * to end, join rnd with sl st in first sc. Fasten off.

Shoulder straps (make 2)

With smallest hook, ch 71 (87, 103).

Rnd 1 Sc in 2nd ch from hook and in next ch, [ch 1, picot, ch 1, sk 2 ch, sc in each of next 2 ch]; rep from [ ] to end of ch, ch 2, working up opposite side of foundation ch, sc in each of first 2 ch, rep from [ ] to end of ch, ch 2, join rnd with sl st in first sc. Fasten off. Stitch straps to upper edge of garment at each point. Weave in all ends. Block.•

BEADED NECKLACE

Melissa Horozewski's single-strand necklace is made by threading chalk turquoise beads onto hemp cord, then positioning the stones as long single-crochet stitches are worked.

••
EASY

SIZE

Instructions are written for one size.

FINISHED MEASUREMENTS

Length approx 45"/114.5cm

MATERIALS

• 1 ball (each approx 650ft/198m) of polished hemp cord, 1mm diameter, 20-lb test (hemp) in natural (www.firemountaingems.com) **1**
• Size D/3 (3.25mm) hook *OR SIZE TO OBTAIN GAUGE*
• Four 15"/38cm strands (approx 14 nuggets per strand) of chalk turquoise medium tumbled nuggets in blue (product #H20-2041KS) from www.firemountaingems.com
• 4"/10cm long bead reamer (product #H20-1590TL) from www.firemountaingems.com
• E-6000® Jewelry and Craft Adhesive
• Toothpick

GAUGE

5 long loop sc to 6"/15cm using size D/3 (3.25mm) hook. *TAKE TIME TO CHECK GAUGE.*

NOTE

Use bead reamer to enlarge holes that are too small to thread.

STITCH GLOSSARY

Long loop sc Draw up a lp on hook to measure 1"/2.5cm, yo and draw through lp on hook, then sc in single strand at back of long loop to lock st.
SLN Slide nugget next to crochet hook.

NECKLACE

String nuggets onto cord, using bead reamer when necessary.

Begin nugget pattern

Make a slip knot, leaving a 4"/10cm tail. Place slip knot on hook.
Rnd 1 Ch 1, *work long loop sc, SLN, draw yarn on hook up to top hole in nugget, ch 1, sc under 2 strands next to nugget; rep from * until all nuggets are used, taking care not to twist necklace, join rnd with a sl st in first sc. Fasten off, leaving a 4"/10cm tail.

FINISHING

Pull on tails to tighten beg slip knot and joining sl st. Use toothpick to apply glue to slip knot and join to secure. Let dry. Cut off excess tails close to sts.•

STAND-ALONE MOTIF

Stitch Key

- • slip stitch (sl st)

- ⬭ chain (ch)

- ┼ single crochet (sc)

- ┬ half double crochet (hdc)

- ⊤ double crochet (dc)

- ⬙ 2-double crochet cluster (2-dc cl)

SHOULDER STRAP

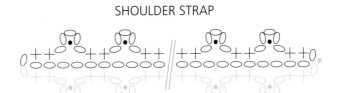

ASSEMBLY DIAGRAM

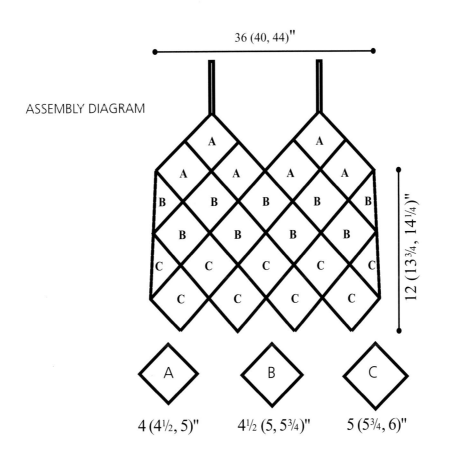

36 (40, 44)"

12 (13¾, 14¼)"

4 (4½, 5)"   4½ (5, 5¾)"   5 (5¾, 6)"

BRUGES BEACH BAG

For this vibrant beach bag, Robyn Chachula chose the Bruges crochet technique, which begins at the center of each motif and works outward in a spiral. This carryall has a solid bottom and is lined with fabric for added structure.

●●●●
COMPLEX

FINISHED MEASUREMENTS
• Width 18"/46cm
• Height 21"/53.5cm

MATERIALS
• 2 3½oz/100g skeins (each approx 430yd/393m) of Lorna's Laces *Shepherd Sock* (superwash wool/nylon) in #1312 cummerbund (red-orange) (1)
• Size E-4 (3.5mm) crochet hook *OR SIZE TO OBTAIN GAUGE*
• Two 8 x 4"/20.5 x 10cm wooden handles
• 1yd/1m of coordinating fabric
• Sewing needle and thread

GAUGE
1 motif = 9 x 4"/23 x 10cm using E/4 (3.5mm) hook.
TAKE TIME TO CHECK GAUGE.

NOTE
Bag is worked in motifs that are connected into strips and then crocheted tog.

STITCH GLOSSARY
ch-5 join Ch 2, sl st to indicated ch-sp, ch 2.

FIRST MOTIF OF EACH STRIP (make 4)
Ch 6.
Row 1 (RS) 3 dc in last ch from hook, turn.
Row 2 Ch 5, 2 dc in first dc, dc in next 2 dc, turn.
Row 3 Ch-5 join to previous ch-sp (1 row below on same end of work), dc in next 4 dc, turn.
Row 4 Ch 5, dc in each dc across, turn.
Rows 5 and 6 Rep rows 3 and 4.
Row 7 Ch-5 join to previous ch-sp, dc in next 3 dc, 2 dc in last dc—5 dc, turn.
Row 8 Rep row 4.
Row 9 Ch-5 join to previous ch-sp, dc in each dc, turn.
Rows 10–16 Rep rows 8 and 9 three times. Rep row 8 once.
Row 17 Ch-5 join to foundation ch used in row 1, dc in each dc, turn.
Row 18 Rep row 4.
Row 19 Ch-5 join to last dc in row 1, dc in each dc, turn.
Row 20 Rep row 4.
Row 21 Ch-5 join to next ch-5 sp on row 2, dc in each dc, turn.
Row 22 Rep row 4.
Row 23 Ch-5 join to same ch-5 sp on row 2, dc in each dc, turn.
Rows 24–39 Rep rows 20–23 four times into rows 4, 6, 8, 10.

Rows 40 and 41 Rep rows 20 and 21 in row 12.
Row 42 Ch-5 join to previous ch-sp on row below, dc in each dc, turn.
Rows 43–45 Ch 5, dc in each dc, turn.
Row 46 Rep row 42.
Rows 47–66 Rep rows 43–46 five times.
Rows 67 and 68 Rep rows 43 and 42.
Rows 69 and 70 Rep rows 43 and 42.
Row 71 Ch-5 join to ch-sp on row 38, dc in each dc, turn.
Row 72 Rep row 42.
Row 73 Ch-5 join to ch-sp on row 40, dc2tog over next 2 dc, dc in next 3 dc—4 dc, turn.
Row 74 Ch-5 join to previous ch-sp on 1 row below, dc in each dc, turn.
Row 75 Ch-5 join to ch-sp on row 44, dc in each dc, turn.
Rows 76–81 Rep rows 74 and 75 three times into rows 48, 52, 56.
Row 82 Ch-5 join to previous ch-sp 1 row below, dc in next 2 dc, dc2tog over next 2 dc—3 dc, turn.
Row 83 Ch-5 join to ch-sp on row 60, dc in each dc, turn.
Row 84 Ch-5 join to previous ch-sp 1 row below, dc3tog over 3 dc, sl st to ch-sp on row 64. Fasten off.

MOTIF STRIPS
(make 4 strips with 4 motifs each)
Join each motif by following motif directions through row 21, then work as foll:
Row 22 Join to ch-sp on row 55 of previous motif, dc in each dc. Ch 5, turn at end of this and every row.
Row 23 Join to same ch-5 sp on row 2, dc in each dc.
Row 24 Join to ch-sp on row 57 of previous motif, dc in each dc. Complete as for motif, fasten off.
Block strips by pinning to size and spraying with water. Allow to dry before continuing.

Joining
Join strips tog by aligning them so the curve of the upper strip's motifs fit into the valley of the lower strip's motifs. Attach yarn to any ch-5 sp with sl st, ch 1, 2 sc in same ch-5 sp, *ch 2, 2 sc in next ch-5 sp on adjoining strip; rep from * across to first ch-sp, ch 2, sl st to first sc. Rep to join all strips together, then join side seam in same way.

Upper edging (make 2)
Ch 10.
Row 1 Dc in 6th ch from hook, and in each ch to end—5 dc, turn.
Row 2 Ch 5, dc in each dc.
Rows 3–5 Rep row 2.

Row 6 Ch-5 join to previous ch-sp 1 row below, dc in each dc. Rep rows 3–6 twice, row 2 once, rows 3–6 twice, row 2 four times, rows 3–6 twice row 2 once, rows 3–6 three times, row 2 once. Fasten off.

Join to top of bag using joining method above, centering on each side of bag and leaving 2½"/6.5cm at each end of each edging unattached. There will be 8"/20.5cm between edgings for handle placement.

Handles

Join yarn around handle by sl st, work backward sc tightly around entire handle to cover. Fasten off. Sew to top of bag between edgings, securing unattached ends of edging to back side of handle.

BASE

Ch 48.

Rnd 1 Dc in 4th ch from hook (sk ch count as dc), dc in next 43 ch, pm, 5 dc in next ch, turn work 180 degrees (beg working in free lp on opposite side of foundation ch), dc in next 43 ch, pm, 4 dc in next ch, sl st to top of t-ch—96 dc.

Note Keep marker between same 2 sts every rnd and sl markers every rnd.

Rnd 2 Ch 3 (counts as 1 dc throughout), dc in base of t-ch (1 st inc'd), dc in each dc to marker, [2 dc in each dc] 5 times, dc in each dc to last marker, [2 dc in each st] 4 times, sl st to top of t-ch—106 dc, 10 sts inc'd.

Rnd 3 Ch 3, dc in base of t-ch, dc in each dc to marker, [2 dc in next dc, dc in next dc] 5 times, dc in each dc to last marker, [2 dc

in next dc, dc in next dc] 4 times, dc to end of rnd, sl st to top of t-ch—116 dc.

Rnd 4 Ch 3, dc in base of t-ch, dc in each dc to marker, [2 dc in next dc, dc in next 2 dc] 5 times, dc in each dc to last marker, [2 dc in next dc, dc in next 2 dc] 4 times, dc to end of rnd, sl st to top of t-ch—126 dc.

Cont in this way, inc 5 sts in each corner, working 1 more dc between incs every rnd, 5 times more—176 dc. Fasten off.

Joining rnd Join yarn to first free ch-sp on right side of any spiral motif at base with sl st, *2 sc in ch-sp, ch 4, sc in 2 dc (on base), [ch 2, 2 sc in next ch-sp (on motif), ch 2, sk 2 dc, sc in next 2 dc] 4 times, ch 4, 2 sc in next ch-sp, ch 5, sk 3 dc, sc in next 2 dc, ch 5, 2 sc in next ch-sp, ch 4, sk 3 dc, sc in next 2 dc, [ch 2, 2 sc in next ch-sp, ch 2, sk 2 dc, sc in next 2 dc] twice, ch 4, sc in next ch-sp, ch 5, sk 3 dc, sc in next 2 dc, ch 5, sk 3 dc; rep from * around, sl st to first sc. Fasten off.

Lining

Cut lining fabric to 37"/94cm wide by 20"/51cm tall, this includes ½"/1.5cm seam allowance. With RS facing, fold lining in half and straight stitch side with ½"/1.5cm seam allowance. Press seam open with iron. Cut lining fabric to 19 x 7"/48 x 17.5cm with rounded corners for bottom. Pin bottom to lining fabric with RS facing. Straight stitch bottom to bag with ½"/1.5cm seam allowance. Press seams to one side, turn right side out. Hem top of bag by pressing ¼"/1cm down twice and straight stitching in place or using hem tape to finish top. Place lining inside of bag. Sew lining inside to top edge of bag along handle and edging.•

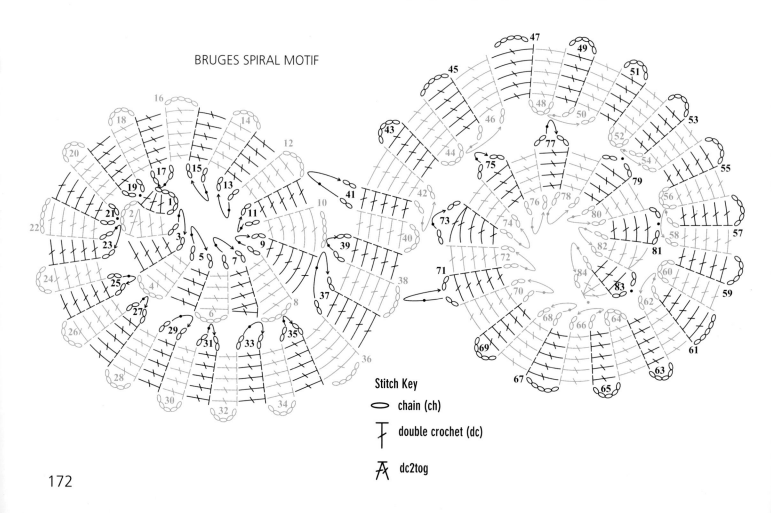

BRUGES SPIRAL MOTIF

Stitch Key

⬭ chain (ch)

⊤ double crochet (dc)

⅄ dc2tog

BRUGES CROCHET HOW-TO

1. Begin Row 9 of the pattern by working a ch-5 join (ch 2, sl st into ch-sp, ch 2) by inserting the hook into the previous chain-space, as shown by the arrow in the motif diagram.

2. At the beginning of row 17, work ch-5 join into the space formed by the foundation chain used in row 1 (see arrow), then work dc in each dc from previous row. Note that we have shown the ch-5 join at the end of row 16, before turning (instead of the beginning of row 17), for clarity.

3. At the beginning of row 19, work ch-5 join into (along side of) the last dc worked in row 1 (see arrow), then work dc in each dc from previous row. Note that we have shown the ch-5 join at the end of row 18, before turning (instead of the beginning of row 19), for clarity.

4. At the beginning of row 21, work ch-5 join into the ch-5 space of row 2 (see arrow), then work dc in each dc from previous row.

5. At the beginning of row 23, work ch-5 join into the same ch-5 space on row 22, then work dc in each dc from previous row.

INDEX